Maid to Queer

Queer Asia

The Queer Asia series opens a space for monographs and anthologies in all disciplines focusing on nonnormative sexuality and gender cultures, identities, and practices across all regions of Asia. Queer studies, queer theory, and transgender studies originated in, and remain dominated by, North American and European academic circles. Yet the separation between sexual orientation and gender identity, while relevant in the West, does not neatly apply to all Asian contexts, which are themselves complex and diverse. Growing numbers of scholars inside and beyond Asia are producing exciting and challenging work that studies Asian histories and cultures of trans and queer phenomena. The Queer Asia series—the first of its kind in publishing—provides a valuable opportunity for developing and sustaining these initiatives.

Selected titles in the series:

Boys' Love, Cosplay, and Androgynous Idols: Queer Fan Cultures in Mainland China, Hong Kong, and Taiwan
Edited by Maud Lavin, Ling Yang, and Jing Jamie Zhao

Contact Moments: The Politics of Intercultural Desire in Japanese Male-Queer Cultures
Katsuhiko Suganuma

Falling into the Lesbi World: Desire and Difference in Indonesia
Evelyn Blackwood

First Queer Voices from Thailand: Uncle Go's Advice Columns for Gays, Lesbians and Kathoeys
Peter A. Jackson

Gender on the Edge: Transgender, Gay, and Other Pacific Islanders
Edited by Niko Besnier and Kalissa Alexeyeff

Obsession: Male Same-Sex Relations in China, 1900–1950
Wenqing Kang

Oral Histories of Older Gay Men in Hong Kong: Unspoken but Unforgotten
Travis S. K. Kong

Queer Politics and Sexual Modernity in Taiwan
Hans Tao-Ming Huang

Queer Chinese Cultures and Mobilities: Kinship, Migration, and Middle Classes
John Wei

Queer Singapore: Illiberal Citizenship and Mediated Cultures
Edited by Audrey Yue and Jun Zubillaga-Pow

Shanghai Lalas: Female Tongzhi Communities and Politics in Urban China
Lucetta Yip Lo Kam

Undercurrents: Queer Culture and Postcolonial Hong Kong
Helen Hok-Sze Leung

Editorial Collective

Chris Berry (King's College London, UK), John Nguyet Erni (Hong Kong Baptist University, Hong Kong), Peter Jackson (Australian National University, Australia), and Helen Hok-Sze Leung (Simon Fraser University, Canada)

International Editorial Board

Dennis Altman (La Trobe University, Australia), Evelyn Blackwood (Purdue University, USA), Tom Boellstorff (University of California, Irvine, USA), Pimpawan Boonmongkon (Mahidol University, Thailand), Judith Butler (University of California, Berkeley, USA), Ding Naifei (National Central University, Taiwan), David Eng (University of Pennsylvania, USA), Neil Garcia (University of the Philippines, Diliman, The Philippines), David Halperin (University of Michigan, Ann Arbor, USA), Josephine Chuen-juei Ho (National Central University, Taiwan), Annamarie Jagose (University of Sydney, Australia), Yinhe Li (Chinese Academy of Social Sciences, China), Song Hwee Lim (The Chinese University of Hong Kong, Hong Kong), Kam Louie (UNSW, Australia), Lenore Manderson (Monash University, Australia), Fran Martin (University of Melbourne, Australia), Mark McLelland (University of Wollongong, Australia), Meaghan Morris (University of Sydney, Australia), Dede Oetomo (University of Surabaya, Indonesia), Cindy Patton (Simon Fraser University, Canada), Ken Plummer (University of Essex, UK), Elspeth Probyn (University of Sydney, Australia), Lisa Rofel (University of California, Santa Cruz, USA), Megan Sinnott (Georgia State University, USA), John Treat (Yale University, USA), Carol Vance (Columbia University, USA), Audrey Yue (National University of Singapore, Singapore)

Maid to Queer

Asian Labor Migration and Female
Same-Sex Desires

Francisca Yuenki Lai

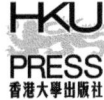

Hong Kong University Press
The University of Hong Kong
Pok Fu Lam Road
Hong Kong
https://hkupress.hku.hk

© 2020 Hong Kong University Press

ISBN 978-988-8528-33-2 (*Hardback*)

All rights reserved. No portion of this publication may be reproduced or transmitted in any form or by any means, electronic or mechanical, including photocopying, recording, or any information storage or retrieval system, without prior permission in writing from the publisher.

British Library Cataloguing-in-Publication Data
A catalogue record for this book is available from the British Library.

Digitally printed

Contents

Acknowledgments	vi
Introduction	1
Chapter 1: Discourses of Home, Gender, and Sexuality	19
Chapter 2: Gender and Sexuality in the Migrant Community	38
Chapter 3: Negotiating Social Positions: Religion, Class, and Race	78
Chapter 4: Imaginings of Home	102
Conclusion	121
References	127
Index	138

Acknowledgments

There are many people whom I owe a great deal of gratitude. First and foremost is my PhD advisor, Evelyn Blackwood. She is my role model, and I hold her in the highest esteem. Her continuous support even after my graduation is crucial to me and has provided hope during the long writing and revision process. My debt of gratitude also goes to the Indonesian migrant women who generously shared their stories. Some of them have become my close friends. There will always be a place for our friendship in this lifetime. I sincerely thank Lucetta Kam for her suggestion of submitting the book manuscript to the Queer Asia series of Hong Kong University Press. I am also grateful to Helen Hok-Sze Leung for her encouragement and positive response to my book proposal at the initial stage.

The book was developed from my PhD dissertation at Purdue University, USA. On the committee, Myrdene Anderson, Patricia Boling, and Ellen Gruenbaum provided me with intellectual guidance and constant encouragement. Sincere thanks go to the Department of Anthropology, Purdue University, for supporting my study and research. I am very thankful to my former colleagues in the Department of Anthropology at the Chinese University of Hong Kong, and in the College of International Education at Hong Kong Baptist University. I want to thank my wonderful colleagues in both the Center for General Education and the College of Humanities and Social Sciences at National Tsing Hua University (NTHU), Taiwan. I especially want to thank my inspiring colleagues in the Institute of Anthropology at NTHU, who invited me to give a talk and provided useful comments on my work. Their warmth and support have definitely eased my transition from Hong Kong to Taiwan.

I want to thank Maria Tam, my master's thesis advisor, for her constant support and believing in my academic work over the past nineteen years. It is she who opened a window of gender studies and anthropological research for me. I would also like to thank Tosa Masaki and Mary Weismantel for their comments on the manuscript and warm encouragement. I am also grateful to the two anonymous reviewers for their comments on the manuscript. Thanks also go to my friends in Hong Kong, Indonesia, and the Philippines. I would like to mention Marrz Balaoro, Catherine "Bun" Chan, Travis Kong, Sky Lau, Phoebe So, Jia Tan, Shiela Tebia, Angel Ting, Day Wong, Lorraine Yeung, Agus, Aya, Fendy, and Janeth.

My parents have provided me all I need. My mother, Leung Yin-Ching, always prioritized my needs above her own. She made no exception even when she was lying in a hospital bed. She passed away in 2014. My mother is my strength and will always be. My sister, Helen Lai, is the greatest sister in the world. She gives me wisdom and is always ready to help before I ask. I am also grateful to my partner, Yannes Ng, for her trust and love, jokes and laughs.

Parts of Chapter 4 have been previously published in "Sexuality at Imagined Home: Same-Sex Desires among Indonesian Migrant Domestic Workers in Hong Kong," *Sexualities* 21 (5–6): 899–913.

Introduction

I attended the Hong Kong Sex Cultural Festival in 2012. One of the themes was the sexuality of ethnic minorities in Hong Kong, including migrant domestic workers who have same-sex relationships. During open floor, a Hong Kong man asked, "Given that these migrant women have a husband in the Philippines or would get married after they return home, can we consider that they are real lesbians?" His question reflects a heteronormative assumption about migrant domestic workers: there should be a reason that migrant workers change their sexual preference while they are in Hong Kong. This way of thinking parallels the gay liberation model, which assumes sexuality is fixed. That is, when a woman changes her sexuality from heterosexual to gay, a possible explanation is that her same-sex desire was suppressed in her earlier years. The lesbian is expected to uphold her lesbian identity for the rest of her life after coming out. This model is incapable of addressing the cultural contexts of migrant domestic workers, not to mention the problem of neglecting the diverse meanings of same-sex relationships to them.

This ethnographic study of Indonesian domestic workers who develop same-sex relationships in Hong Kong therefore aims to create a dialogue between Asian labor migration and lesbian and queer studies. On the one hand, Asian labor migration studies has a strong focus on how the global trends in the feminization of labor migration have shaped the meaning and practices of transnational family and motherhood. However, the research themes on family and motherhood have markedly neglected lesbian workers and other alternative family forms and relations. On the other hand, queer studies often ignores the situations of low-skilled migrant workers who develop same-sex relationships during their stay in their host country. This book examines and inquiries about the struggles and concerns of migrant workers and their changing notions of family and marriage in migratory processes. How do these ideas shape the gender and sexual subjectivities of Indonesian women in Hong Kong?

The Indonesian women in this book do not articulate a desire for same-sex relationships before migrating. My work contrasts the Indonesian migrant experiences of same-sex relationships in Hong Kong with the discourse of western sexual identity, which assumes that individuals have a strong sense of sexual identification prior to migration. For example, in the work of two prominent scholars, Martin Manalansan (2003) and Lionel Cantú (2009), the migrants have already identified themselves as gay or sexually interested in men before they migrated to the United States. Their fear of coming out and experiences of marginalization in their home country partly constitute their motivations for moving to the States. This notion unintentionally implies that there is a "real" sexual orientation to pursue. By examining the Asian female migrant experience with same-sex relationships, I argue that same-sex desires are not necessarily realized before migration and pursued by leaving home; instead, the migratory processes *enable* individuals to articulate a desire for same-sex relationships and engage in them.

The book enriches queer migration studies by offering a gender perspective and elucidating how female live-in domestic workers develop same-sex relationships even though they are deprived of the right of mobility at night and are subjected to gendered moral expectations. Queer migration studies have shown that gay male migrants can navigate space in the city despite sometimes feeling racially marginalized. Their male identity grants them mobility to go to cruising areas at night. My work is directed at the unquestioned male privilege of gay migrants by examining the spatial significance of how migrant same-sex relationships are developed under the gendered moral expectations and constraints of female live-in domestic workers.

Labor Migration and Sexuality

Among the studies that focus on the sexuality of migrant women during their stay in their host country, migrant women present themselves as "good women" in an attempt to make sense of their sexual behaviors that deviate from heteronormative expectations. Johan Lindquist studied how some of the Indonesian women who migrated to Batam, an Indonesian island near Singapore, end up as sex workers after losing their job in the factories. The women feel obligated to fulfill the cultural expectation of returning home with money; therefore, they turn to sex work (Lindquist 2009a). Ford and Lyons (2008) also studied how Indonesian women use sex work as a means of class mobility. These women maintain their identities at home as "good mothers" and "dutiful daughters" by sending home money to their children and parents. Yet ironically, their notions of home and strong family bonds have compelled them to engage in sex work for quick money. Although they have violated sexual norms, they still see themselves as moral people and good women because they strive to make money (albeit illicitly) to fulfill the expectations of daughters and mothers. Their notion of a "good woman" is ambiguous and cannot be defined simply by legitimate sexual behavior; rather, they consider more crucial whether their distant home and family members perceive them as dutiful daughters or good mothers.

The above studies clearly demonstrate the agency and intentionality of migrant women workers when they deviate from sexual norms. However, their pleasure and romance have been neglected when sexuality is portrayed as a means of reaping monetary rewards. Amy Sim (2009) calls for academic attention to the nonwork experiences of migrant domestic workers and their response to the need for sex and love. How do migrant women workers manage to develop romantic relationships and obtain pleasure in their host cities?

Lan Anh Hoang and Brenda Yeoh (2015), in their study of Vietnamese migrant women in Taiwan, documented the complexities and ambivalence that characterized the love and sexual lives of the Vietnamese migrant women. Fulfillment of love and sexual desire is usually accompanied by economic considerations, whether migrant women decided to enter an extramarital relationship or not. Nicole Constable observed in her monograph that despite warnings, some migrant domestic workers in Hong Kong have relationships with men or develop same-sex relationships. Constable (2014) pointed out that Hong Kong is a liminal space to these migrant workers: there are sexual norms that migrant workers are supposed to follow, but the fact is, there are no immediate consequences if they do not. Therefore, migrant workers have more freedom to act on temptation and desires while struggling with notions of being good women, especially in relation to their seemingly conflicting roles as wife and mother.

In her study on Indonesian migrant domestic workers in Hong Kong, Amy Sim (2009) offered multiple reasons for *why* these women change their sexual preference from men to women in the migratory process. The women are lonely and need an emotion outlet when they find out that their husband is involved in an affair; they know that lesbianism would not result in pregnancy and therefore can protect their moral universe. While Sim attempts to explain why heterosexual women would engage in a same-sex relationship in Hong Kong, her explanation falls short of contextualizing the stories of the women, particularly how they change their notions of gender and sexuality, including how they ascribe meaning to same-sex relationships and their perceptions of lesbianism shift from anomaly to normalcy and from impossible to possible.

As noted by scholars in both transnational feminism and queer migration studies, migration is an active process of creating subjectivities. Inderpal Grewal and Caren Kaplan (2001) noted that contacts and transactions of travel are part of the knowledge production that constitutes and creates new subjects. Hector Carillo (2004) coined the term "sexual migration," which suggests that transnational movement enables queer practices, identities, and subjectivities. In his study on gay men in the United States, Nathaniel Lewis proposed the notion of "migration prompting personal reassessment" to understand the role of migration in shaping the expression of sexual identity. He argues that migration gives gay men the opportunity to distance themselves from heterosexual relationships and realize the possibility of a different life. The gay men in his study had long been aware of their sexual interest in men, but did not consider disclosing their gay identity until given the opportunity to relocate. The adoption of a gay identity is an accretive process in which these gay men reconsider their sexuality along with their marriage, career path, and family during the several alternating trips between their current home and potential queer home. That is, the process is not a one-time undertaking but a gradual and accretive process (Lewis 2012).

The idea of migration shaping sexuality is very useful for analyzing the sexual subjectivity of Indonesian migrant women. My work not only examines how Indonesian women negotiate the sexual ideologies of Indonesia and Hong Kong but also how migrant labor policies and the practices of Hong Kong people unintentionally produce alternative sexualities and desires.

Maid, Queer, and Heteronormativity

Maid to Queer aims to highlight the changes of subject positions of Indonesian women from live-in maid to a nonnormative position in the gender/sexuality system. This book addresses the conflicting discourses about the moral standards of Indonesian women and the many social processes that enable them to experience sexual fluidity and perceive themselves *otherwise*—different from what they think about themselves before leaving home. I use "queer" as a subject position, a nonnormative position in which these Indonesian women negotiate heteronormativity while drawing meaning from it to live on. Queer is not used as an identity in the book because the Indonesian women in this study do not identify themselves as queer people.

It is important to clarify that "sexual fluidity" is not a synonym for "bisexuality." In her study of female sexual fluidity, Lisa Diamond (2008) interviewed more than one hundred middle-class women from both urban and rural sites in the United States. She argued that women possess a capacity for fluidity in addition to their sexual orientation. While "sexual orientation" refers to the gender of the people one is mainly attracted to, "sexual fluidity" refers to sexual attraction that is not aligned with a person's sexual orientation. This sexual attraction can be triggered by relationships and situations; for example, an intense emotional relationship with either a man or a woman or moving to a place that provides positive experiences with same-sex relationships. Diamond's notion of sexual fluidity enables us to understand that sexual attraction is not merely determined by sexual orientation. She also reminds us that sexual attraction and fluidity is *not* a matter of choice. Some women in her study reported that they actively resisted the changes but in vain. Following Diamond, my study does not take sexuality as a kind of fixity; instead, I ask how sexual desires are produced and sustained in relation to their subject positions and the contexts the Indonesian women find themselves in.

There are debates as to whether a queer perspective is suitable for analyzing sexual subjectivities that do not publicly denounce heteronormativity and that are outside Euro-American locations (see also Boellstorff 2007; Lewin 2016). In a retrospective paper, Margot Weiss (2016) challenged queerness as a prescriptive project, as it assumes that queer objects are antinormative. Saskia Wieringa (2015) also criticized queer studies for uncritically assuming all people who live a nonheteronormative life are queer. Both question the reinforcement of "simple dichotomies between heterosexual and everything queer" (Weiss 2016, 632). Furthermore, queer studies has been taken to task for overlooking the diversity among queer people of different races, genders, religions, and social classes. Feminist critics have long called queer studies to account for prioritizing the experience of white, middle-class gay men in Euro-American urban locations and overlooking the specificities of contexts in which lesbians, bisexual, and transgender people are situated (Wieringa, Bhaiya, and Katjasungkana 2015).

Responding to these criticisms, queer scholars strive to produce new works that are attentive to the power dimensions of race, class, and gender that shape queer lives; the paradox of the regulatory regimes that shape both marginalization and resistance; and the complex negotiations of normativity (Engebretsen 2014). Martin Manalansan argues for a "new queer studies" (2003, 7) that is mindful of the politics of location brought by colonization, postcolonization, and transnational migration. His approach aims to illuminate "the different ways in which queer subjects located in and moving in between specific national locations establish and negotiate complex relationships to each other and to the state" (2003, 8). Lisa Duggan's idea of homonormativity (2002) also expanded the discussion of normativity in queer studies by seeing how normativity works with neoliberalism. People in nonheterosexual relationships are not inherently subversive; they become "normal" by complying with neoliberal values, such as commitment to monogamous relationships and stable jobs.

A queer analytic approach is still very useful for analyzing transgression and normativity, for examining sexual subjectivities in a transnational migratory context. I use a queer lens to highlight (1) the heteronormative policies and practices in labor migration and the structured inequalities imposed on queer migrants (Cantú 2009), (2) the instability and subversion of heteronormativity when individuals resist and negotiate these norms and regulations (Blackwood and Johnson 2012), and (3) the "productive possibilities" of queerness and norm—queerness is not about heroic distancing from the normative but rather how the two constantly intersect and reconstitute, because norm and queer are not easily separable (Manalansan 2018, 1288). The notion of productive possibilities is powerful for rethinking how queer people construct their norms without isolating themselves from the mainstream, heteronormative world out of which they also draw social meanings to live on. My work examines the linkages between heteronormativity, racialization, Islamic regulations, and the specificity of domestic work to understand the reconstitution of normativity by Indonesian women in a migratory context.

Heteronormativity is not equivalent to heterosexuality but refers to a wide range of practices and institutions that inform the normative daily life; it shapes the lives of members of society and produces effects upon those who comply with these expectations as well as those who fall outside of its norms (Jackson 2006; Wieringa 2015). Heteronormativity is not monolithic but always negotiable and productive of shifting meanings and diverse effects upon different individuals. For instance, gay is becoming "normal" as gay men openly show their willing commitment to heteronormative ideals, such as maintaining a monogamous relationship. Since heteronormativity is by no means absolute but negotiable, Wieringa (2015) argues for an intersectional lens to examine how the dimensions of gender, race, class, and religion shape these negotiation processes, which are filled with dilemmas of choosing between acceptance and resistance, and to investigate the diverse effects of heteronormativity on individual bodies. Adopting an intersectional lens, this book takes on two different subject positions, *maid* and *queer*, to examine how Indonesian women negotiate heteronormativity and reconstitute it in relation to gender, race, religion, and the specificity of domestic work.

Migrant Community and Same-Sex Desires

Evelyn Blackwood and Saskia Wieringa have written extensively on queer female bodies in Indonesia since the publication of their edited anthology *Female Desires* in 1999. Not only do they provide a thick description of how female queer bodies negotiate heteronormative gender ideology and marriage pressure in Indonesia; both scholars also address the globalization of LGBT identities and its effects on queer individuals in Asia, such as obscuring sexual meanings outside the LGBT model (Blackwood and Wieringa 2007). In her study on *tomboi* (the Indonesian term for "tomboy") in Padang, in the West Sumatra Province of Indonesia, Blackwood notes the intersection of global LGBT knowledge and identity-based communities in Indonesia, particularly how the erratic circulation of queer discourses between the capital city (Jakarta) and less developed regional cities (Padang in her study) shape the sexual subjectivities of the working-class *tomboi* and their girlfriends. She uses the "asymmetries of queer knowledge" to explain the uniqueness of *tomboi* subjectivity, which differs from the lesbian subjectivity embodied by the activists who are living in Jakarta (Blackwood 2010: 205).

My research, which is inspired by Blackwood's study on the distinctiveness of *tomboi* subjectivity, examines group-based interactions in the migrant community and investigates the ways these daily interactions shape and influence how Indonesian women perceive masculinity, femininity, and same-sex relationships. I am also inspired by Marlon Bailey (2013), who conducted research on butch queens and ballroom culture among the black community in Detroit in the United States. Close friends form ballroom houses that produce competitive live performance events. These houses are reconstitutions of the homes that rejected these queer people as they transform friendships into kin relations of parents and children. Fictive kin terms are commonly used among this community. Therefore, acts of creating kin and kin labor provide social support and offer a safe haven from homophobic violence. While I am aware that there is no direct cultural connection between the ballroom houses in Detroit and the social groups formed by Indonesian migrant workers in Hong Kong, Bailey's notion of kin labor is useful for examining the fictive family networks these migrant workers establish among themselves in Hong Kong, as well as how their fictive home and kin relations shape their gender and sexual subjectivities.

Intersectionality and Negotiating Social Positions

Queer migration scholarship flourished in the first decade of the twenty-first century, and one of its academic accomplishments is having enriched the concept of sexuality by accounting for the intersectionality of race and noncitizenship and the ways that the social position of queer migrants affects their sexuality (Cantú 2009; Manalansan 2003; Luibhéid 2008). It also addressed the role of geographical space, the movement across borders, and navigating the spaces of migrant communities or the home of the employer in producing identity and subjectivity (Valentine 2007). Queer migrants face structural inequality that may produce experiences and lifestyles that differ from those of lesbian and gay citizens. In his study of Filipino gay men in New York City, Manalansan (2003) addresses how racism there shaped their lived experiences. For example, they refrained from cruising in white areas, even though public cruising is supposed to be a democratic practice. In response, gay migrants from Asia and South America found their own cruising area. However, Filipino gay men still feel vulnerable there because public sex acts expose them to arrest and deportation. While police seldom arrest gay citizens for public sex acts, this is not true of gay migrants. Therefore, their racial identity and noncitizenship eclipse their gay identity in the United States. The idea of public cruising as a democratic practice does not apply to gay migrants at all.

The gender identity of queer migrants may outweigh their sexual identity when the patriarchal context is taken into consideration. Oliva Espín addresses the intersectionality of gender and sexuality in her study of Latina lesbians in the United States. In a patriarchal context, the sexuality of daughters represents the honor of her family. Espín notes that the struggle of immigrant families to acculturate frequently centers on the sexual behavior of daughters, as many immigrant communities perceive "to be Americanized" as almost synonymous with sexual promiscuity. Among immigrant communities, girls and women are expected to continue living as though they were still in the old country, but young men are encouraged to develop a new identity (Espín 1996). Espín's work sheds light on the constraints, particularly familial surveillance, that lesbian migrants encounter in a new country. Her argument highlights the need for special attention to the gender position of lesbian migrants and the moral expectations imposed upon women.

The intersectionality of race, class, and gender is salient to live-in domestic workers who usually have no coworkers or support in addressing issues with their employer. Previous studies of migrant domestic workers have pointed out their marginalized position in the employer's home, which is a place of racial, class, and gender oppression (Constable 1997; Ehrenreich and Hochschild 2002; Yeoh and Huang 2010). Nicole Constable (1997) delineated how Hong Kong employers controlled the gender appearance of migrant domestic workers with the underlying assumption that their youth and beauty constitute a sexual threat. Household rules included a prohibition on tight clothing, dresses, or makeup being worn at home. For example, one of the interviewed Filipino domestic workers was very upset when her employer cut her shoulder-length hair in a short man's style without her consent.

Departing from Constable's study, my research takes the forced haircut as the starting point of investigation and not the end. Would a migrant domestic worker reconsider her sexuality after a significant change of gender appearance? I ask this question because Indonesian migrant domestic workers are not isolated from the migrant community. A man's haircut could mean something desirable or mark its wearer as a lesbian in the migrant community. Therefore, I explore how Indonesian migrant domestic workers modify their gender appearance in accordance with the gendered expectations in the home of their employer while drawing on the meaning of female masculinity in the migrant community. The home of the employer is not merely about race and class oppression but might become a space for producing an alternative masculinity and sexuality.

Another way to consider the social position of women workers in the migratory process is the intersectionality of religion, class, and sexuality. Previous studies on migrant domestic workers and Islam have addressed how the perceived low status of live-in maids has become an excuse for employers to violate their religious rights, including forcing Muslim workers to consume pork, which is forbidden in Islamic law, and denying them the right to pray (for an obligatory five times a day) or wear a *jilbab* (headscarf), which is a symbolic part of female Islamic dress that demonstrates modesty.[1]

---

1. There is a wide spectrum of Islamic clothing for women in Indonesia. It ranges from the nearly all-black, Saudi-associated styles with face coverings, to colorful and often fitted styles with a headscarf called a *jilbab* (Jones 2007).

Instead of viewing this type of treatment as merely another form of class oppression and discrimination, both Paul O'Connor (2012) and Nicole Constable (2011) point out that the involuntary violation of the Islamic principles provide migrant women a break from and opportunity to reflect on their religious beliefs. An Indonesian informant told O'Connor that she decided to "dress sexy" when she found it difficult to follow Islamic rules because her employer did not allow her to pray at home or wear a *jilbab*. The worker also noted that Indonesian women should not be faulted for failing to observe Islamic rules in Hong Kong, as "it is the circumstances that they find themselves in" (O'Connor 2012, 50). Constable (2011) also noted that migrant women use "oppressive employer" as an excuse to disregard religious expectations, such as consuming pork or not praying.

The space and freedom in Hong Kong allow migrant women to reflect on their religion and expectations imposed on women. Constable (2011) notes that her Indonesian Muslim informants become more critical of their faith after leaving Indonesia. However, being critical of Islam does not necessarily mean abandoning Islam. Eni Lestari, one of her informants, noted the growth of conservative Islam in Hong Kong since 2004. Eni became aware of the infiltration of conservative Islam into the Indonesian migrant community in Hong Kong through the emergence of "moral police" who condemned women who spoke up or engaged in a lesbian relationship. Eni established Gabungan Migran Muslim Indonesia (Indonesian Migrant Muslim Alliance, GAMMI) to encourage Indonesian women to dialogue and become leaders by recasting the roots of Islam as liberating and revolutionary. To Eni and the GAMMI members, the weight of Muslim identity has not been reduced but is salient in the migratory process.

The above shows the transformation of religious subjectivity in the process of migration. The Muslim identity might become less important or more salient, depending on the migratory experiences and the situations that these women find themselves in. I will examine how the Indonesian women perceive their Muslim identity and religious faith when they are unable to follow the religious rules in Hong Kong. With a changing and negotiable definition of religious piety, how do they reconcile their same-sex desires with Muslim identity?

Asian Family and Queer Imaginings of Home

Lesbian and queer studies seek to destabilize the notion of home and domesticity and explore the formation of a plurality of identities and subjective experiences (Pilkey, Scicluna, and Gorman-Murray 2015). Previous studies have illustrated the plurality of queer subjectivity by demonstrating how queer individuals negotiate heteronormative expectations and the pressure to marry and simultaneously improvise strategies to maintain their same-sex sexuality and relationships. Manalansan (2003) documents how Filipino gay men use silence as a strategy when they reveal their gay identity to their parents, which contrasts Asian queer subjectivity with the Western discourse of "coming out" to their family members. Studies on Indonesian lesbians by Saskia Wieringa (2007) and Evelyn Blackwood (2010) also show that Indonesian lesbians do not expect their family members or neighbors to acknowledge their same-sex relationships even though they might have their suspicions. Tom Boellstorff (1999) argues that the Indonesian gay men in his study do not necessarily perceive heterosexuality and homosexuality as an "either/or" proposition, as defined in the gay liberation model, since they balance both heterosexual marriage and a gay relationship at the same time.

Unlike their LGBT counterparts in the above studies, the Indonesian women in this book are physically distant from their home. Therefore, they are less often subjected to confrontations with their parents over their potential same-sex sexuality. Nevertheless, these studies are still relevant to the discussion on the sexual subjectivity of the migrant workers in terms of the notion of home, especially how they manage their relationship with their parents, who would normally expect their daughters to return home and marry before they become "too old." Although the women are physically distant from their parents, they are still expected to fulfill the role of a "dutiful daughter" by calling their parents regularly. They are also supposed to return to Indonesia to visit their parents during the two-week leave between old and new contracts. While the heteronormative surveillance is at a physical remove, the women still face pressure when they speak to their parents on the phone or return home during holidays.

Martin Manalansan calls for extending migration studies beyond normative and universalized family patterns. Manalansan (2006) is critical of the dominant focus of the "chain of care" in labor migration studies on transnational motherhood with excessive emphasis on the heterosexual family. He points out that stories of single women and lesbians are often sidelined in favor of those of migrant mothers. Echoing Manalansan, my work infuses the traditional definition of family and home in migration studies with a new perspective. I do not perceive family and home as mere physical entities; instead, I expand family and home to include their imaginings of home. I examine how these imaginings shape the meanings of their same-sex relationships and their sexual subjectivity in a transnational context.

Arjun Appadurai (1996) notes that imagination has acquired a new power in a transnational world and considers its implications for doing ethnography:

> Ethnographers can no longer simply be content with the thickness they bring to the local. . . . For what is real about ordinary lives is now real in many ways that range from the sheer contingency of individual lives . . . to the realisms that individuals are exposed to and draw on their daily lives. These complex, partly imagined lives must now form the bedrock of ethnography. . . . [E]thnography must redefine itself as that practice of representation that

illuminates the power of large-scale, imagined life possibilities over specific life trajectories. (1996, 54–55)

Appadurai emphasizes that ethnographers must attend to projected imaginations because they encourage the pursuit of certain lifestyles and contribute to new life meanings. Appadurai (2002) also states that imagination is not mere fantasy but a form of social practice and negotiation. That is, people negotiate their current state of affairs and their imagined future life. Rather than viewing imagination as constraint-free and completely boundless, Appadurai argues for a focus on specific life trajectories, because they are the essence of meaningful imaginations. Following Appadurai, I examine the imagined life possibilities of the Indonesian women in relation to their life trajectories and gender expectations in Indonesia.

The imaginings of home are crucial for understanding the sexual subjectivity of migrant domestic workers as they alternate between the pleasure they obtain from same-sex relationships in Hong Kong and the social constraints imposed on them, and the negotiations between Indonesian migrant women and the larger society in Indonesia. Negotiation does not mean that the Indonesian women abandon their family back home. I examine how memories of home and migratory experiences both within and outside of Indonesia constitute their imaginings of home and consider how their same-sex desires and compliance with heteronormative expectations intertwine in these imaginings.

Research Questions

This book examines the migratory experiences and sexual subjectivity of Indonesian migrant workers during the many transnational processes of (1) leaving their home in Indonesia and maintaining physical distance to evade the gaze of their parents, (2) establishing a migrant community with other Indonesian domestic workers in Hong Kong, (3) adapting to a racist and heterosexist environment in Hong Kong, and (4) projecting their imaginings of home in Indonesia. The following questions will be addressed in this book:

- What are the gender and sexual subjectivities (including thoughts, struggles, and actions) of Indonesian migrant workers who have developed same-sex relationships in Hong Kong?
- What gender and sexual knowledge has been produced by the migrant community in Hong Kong that enables its members to engage in same-sex relationships?
- How do their imaginings of home produce meaning in their same-sex relationships in Hong Kong despite their inevitable return to Indonesia?

Field Methods

To understand the formation of sexual subjectivity and how migrant workers make sense of their same-sex relationships in Hong Kong, I adopted a qualitative and ethnographic approach, which relies on conversations, participant observation, and formal interviews to collect the stories of migrant workers, including their views of migration and home, as well as the meanings of same-sex relationships to them. Their stories are crucially important to this research because ordinary people (like the average migrant worker in this study) make sense of their life and realize the world through their daily experiences (Parreñas 2001). Sexual subjectivity can be observed in daily life practices through gender expression, dating style and practices, and behaviors that reproduce or negotiate gender and sexual regimes (Blackwood and Wieringa 2007).

As an ethnographer, I immersed myself in the Sunday life of Indonesian women where they socialized: parks, beaches, malls, food venues, a learning center operated by a Christian church, and monthly rental rooms from October 2010 to July 2012. I observed how individuals and couples presented themselves in a group setting, including their clothing, hairstyle, and accessories, and their interactions through conversations, body movement, and division of labor between the masculine and feminine genders. I also went shopping and had dinner with individual women and couples. Spending time with them individually allowed casual and personal conversations about their life back in Indonesia and now in Hong Kong, such as where they shopped for clothes, as well as where they felt comfortable enough to spend their holidays with their girlfriend.

In addition, I participated in their formal activities, for example, a fashion show organized by the migrant workers themselves. In doing so, I was categorized according to their binary gender system as a *tomboi*. A detailed discussion of this will follow in Chapter 2. I also maintained contact with these migrant workers through SMS and Facebook on the weekdays when they had to work. Facebook served as an additional channel for observing their social networking and uploaded photos.

Apart from joining their Sunday activities, I also accompanied some of the migrant workers to employment agencies and the Labour Department office to settle their labor disputes on the weekdays. This wide range of experiences provided a holistic view to place their gender and sexuality stories within a broader social context, particularly how migrant policy and class and race hierarchies shape the sexual subjectivities of women.

Structured interviews were carried out when a trusting relationship had been established with individual migrant workers. The following topics were incorporated into the in-depth interviews: (1) their thoughts, aspirations, and ideal life paths in terms of family, career, and relationships, including both heterosexual and same-sex relationships; (2) their life in Indonesia, including all gender-related experiences at home and school, in the workplace, and at the training center; (3) their relationships with their Hong Kong employers and the gendered expectations of them as live-in domestic workers; (4) their motivations for joining the pop dance group and their thoughts about the gendered costumes and performances; (5) their knowledge of a homosocial romantic discourse in popular culture and the sexual rights movement in Indonesia and Hong Kong; and (6) the ways that they deal with the pressure to marry and conflicts with religious beliefs.

While I was carrying out my research, I was also aware of my privilege in the field—I sat with these Indonesian women and documented their lives and stories. Therefore, I also sought opportunities to contribute to their activities, including taking and photofinishing pictures of their birthday parties, mixing songs for their dance practice sessions with computer software, teaching English classes at Victoria Park, and helping them with English or Cantonese communication with other parties.

Entering the Community

In August 2010, I contacted a labor union formed by Indonesian migrant domestic workers in Hong Kong. I told them about my research topic on same-sex relationships among Indonesian migrant women. Through their network, I was introduced to a *moderen* (modern) dance group, a name they used to emphasize their difference from Indonesian traditional dancing. They mixed dance-pop, hip-hop, and break-dance moves. To avoid confusing them with the genre of modern dance, I refer them as pop dance groups in the rest of the book. I was first introduced to a pop dance group, Champion (a pseudonym), in October 2010. I was fascinated by the visibility of female same-sex relationships among the members. Champion has thirty active members, and the number of *tomboi* and *cewek* (girls) are about the same. I instinctively knew that Champion would be an ideal group for my research purpose, as my focus was on their same-sex relationships.

I disclosed both my research purpose as well as my lesbian identity when I first met the Indonesian labor union and then the pop dance group. My coming-out decision to the informants was supported by previous field projects in lesbian, gay, and queer studies, in which the ethnographers found that revealing their sexual identity to their informants greatly facilitated their admission into the community, as the informants were relieved to share a common sexual identity with the researchers (Blackwood 2010; Kong 2010; Lewin and Leap 1996). My overtness in disclosing my dual identities as both a researcher and a lesbian greatly eased my entry into the migrant community despite our differences in race and class. My informants were generally willing to talk to me about their same-sex relationships based on our shared identity.

After spending two consecutive Sundays with Champion, I asked the leader for permission to conduct research with her group. She was receptive, and I became an official member of Champion after two months. My membership card, T-shirt uniform printed with Champion and my first name, and monthly payment officially marked my membership, although I did not dance as vigorously as the other members. Through Champion, I became acquainted with more Indonesian migrant women and members of other dance groups.

I met with the Champion members mostly at Kowloon Park or Victoria Park. Their official meeting time was from 2:00 in the afternoon to 5:00 in the evening. They held various activities during those three hours apart from dancing, for example, participating in formal performance events, meeting with labor unions, or holding internal meetings. I also spent time with them before and after their official meetings. My first in-depth interview did not occur until July 2011. Since I could meet with them only once a week, on Sundays, nine months lapsed before I established sufficient trust to commence in-depth interviews.

Indonesian is my third language, after Chinese and English. I attended two intensive language courses, one in the United States (at the Southeast Asian Studies Summer Institute, held at the University of Wisconsin–Madison) and one in Indonesia (Alam Bahasa, a private language school in Yogyakarta) in the summers of 2010 and 2011, respectively. During my fieldwork and in-depth interviews, I used Indonesian to communicate with the Indonesian women. I also used Cantonese (a Chinese dialect spoken in Hong Kong and southern China) and English when I did not know how to express certain ideas in Indonesian. My informants could speak either Cantonese or English or both. However, their spoken Cantonese or English was not as fluent as that of native speakers. During our conversations, we switched between the three languages whenever we thought that we could communicate more effectively in that language.

Researcher's Sexuality in the Field

I was in my early thirties when I started this fieldwork. New acquaintances often mistake me for a man based on my gender appearance: I have short hair around the ears and wear men's clothing. I came out to my informants as a lesbian and told them that I was in a stable relationship with a Hong Kong woman. They asked me for pictures of my girlfriend, whose feminine appearance reinforced their assumption of my gender position as a *tomboi* because a *tomboi* pairs up with a feminine woman. My presence in the field reinforced the construction of the same-sex culture of the Indonesian migrant community, in which a *tomboi* is paired with a feminine woman. My girlfriend met my informants only a few times. Over two years of fieldwork, I was on my own, without her. I spent time with the Indonesian women, I ate with them, and I learned and spoke the same language. I wanted to be a part of their community and be treated the same.

Same-sex attractions and romantic relationships are important dimensions of the lives of these community members. Inevitably, I was also seen as an object of desire there.

In December 2010, I began to mingle with the members of Champion every Sunday in the park. One of the members was Ria, a twenty-year-old with a feminine appearance and shoulder-length hair. She liked to spend time with me and talk, because I was the only friend with whom she can practice her English. She helped translate Indonesian to English at times when I did not fully understand the conversations of the group members. Her willingness to act as my translator made my presence in the migrant community less awkward and more engaging. Although I equipped myself with basic Indonesian before beginning my fieldwork, my language skills were still insufficient for understanding everyday dialogue spoken at a normal speed. Ria facilitated my engagement in their social circles. When we spent time alone, Ria shared many of her own stories and the gossip of other Champion members, for example, rumored couples.

About a month later, I went to meet with the group as I usually did in the park. I saw Ria from a distance, and as I walked toward her, she suddenly hid behind another person, looking embarrassed. I was confused about her reaction. Her friend told me, "She likes you." At that moment, it dawned on me that I was positioned as not only a researcher but also an object of desire in the field. As noted by Evelyn Blackwood, researchers "occupy multiple positions and identities that transform over time, forcing us constantly to reconstruct who we are in relation to the people we study" (1995, 55).

One day, Ria told me that many of her friends thought that we were in a relationship. She said that she did not mind because she did not want to be viewed as a single woman but someone with a *tomboi* partner. She said the Champion members would gossip about her whenever she was close to a *tomboi*, even if there was not any romantic connotation. Now that there were rumors that Ria and I were in a relationship, Ria used this misconception to her advantage, to prevent gossip when she formed a closer relationship with other *tomboi* in Champion. Ria showed no intention of clarifying our relationship to the Champion members. My response to Ria was that the Champion members should already know that I had a girlfriend. About three months later, Ria told me that she fell in love with a *tomboi* and showed me their pictures. I was relieved because I was not her object of desire anymore.

Unlike most other anthropologists conducting fieldwork in a foreign country, I lived with my girlfriend in my hometown. I was very sure that I did not want a romantic relationship with Ria. I was not attracted to her sexually. But I liked spending time with her, as she was a happy, energetic, chatty young woman. I liked Ria being close to me because her presence could facilitate my communication with other Indonesian women in the research process. Yet I was vigilant about negotiating the two identities of a researcher and a *tomboi*. As a researcher,

I spent time with Ria because she always had stories to share with me. Through our conversations, I learned how these Indonesian women made sense of their gender and same-sex relationships. As a *tomboi*, I was aware of Ria's interest in me and I also enjoyed spending time with her. While I reminded myself that I should avoid any conversation that would lead Ria to think that I was attracted to her, I did not avoid spending time with Ria alone; for instance, I still asked Ria to have lunch or dinner with me.

I recalled a methodology graduate seminar that I attended in early 2000s about insiders conducting fieldwork. It considered how an insider identity might ease entry into a community when the informants found a common identity with the ethnographer. However, how ethnographers should handle their own romantic or sexual relationships in the field was not fully addressed. My experience in graduate school was not unique. Don Kulick (1995) noted that anthropologists remain very tight lipped about their own sexuality despite decades of concern with the sex lives of others. Kulick urged anthropologists to recognize and reflect on their desire and erotic subjectivity as the reflexive process would help them critically examine their privileged positions in the field (i.e., recording the romantic and sex stories of others without sharing their own) and reveal their self-protective motive behind remaining celibate: to protect their academic career rather than their informants. Anthropologists who have sexual relations with informants risk being stamped as "unethical" for taking advantage of their informants; it might endanger their professional identity and academic career (Kulick 1995; Wekker 2006).

In reflecting on how I negotiated the two identities of researcher and *tomboi*, I confess that I feared a romantic relationship with Ria (or any member of the migrant community) because it would threaten my professional identity. At the same time, I also feared losing our close friendship that eased my presence in the community. For me, not indulging in a romantic relationship with any member of the migrant community was not a matter of ethics but more a matter of professional consequences. As noted by Jill Dubisch, "We 'use' them to further our goals, writing and speaking in public contexts about personal and even intimate aspects of their lives, appropriating these lives for our own professional purposes. Could a sexual relationship be any more intimate, committing, or exploitative than our normal relations with the 'natives'? Or is it really ourselves we are trying to protect?" (1995, 31). As a matter of ethics, I should consider Ria's feelings and maintain a professional distance, at least not asking her to lunch or dinner alone. Reflecting on Dubisch's question, I confess that I weighted my professional career over Ria's feelings.

But it is an oversimplification to assume that I had power over Ria. In delineating her sexual relationship with her informant in Suriname, Wekker (2006) found that she did not have more power over her informant lover despite her middle-class status (i.e., being a PhD candidate) and lighter skin color. Instead, culture and age matter more in the working-class Surinamese context. Informants are also active agents and can have equal or even more power than anthropologists in the field. In reviewing my relationship with Ria, she had some control over rumors about us because she did not clarify our relationship to others but instead took the advantage of the rumors to counter gossip directed at her. I found that my position in Champion, as a rumored lover of Ria, was out of my control.

Profile of the Indonesian Women

I collected life stories from forty-three Indonesian women in Hong Kong. They include that of nineteen *cewek* and twenty-four *tomboi* between the ages of twenty and thirty-nine. The median age was twenty-seven. All were from the island of Java, except two from the islands of Sulawesi and Sumbawa. In terms of education level, two had completed primary school (*sekolah dasar*); twenty-two had completed middle school (*sekolah menengah pertama*), eighteen had completed high school (*sekolah menengah atas*), and one had completed college and received her degree (*stratum satu*). All were Muslim except for two Christians. One of the Christians was from Sulawesi.

Fifteen of the forty-three women were or had been married. Among the fifteen married women, one was a widow and two were divorced. The remaining twelve indicated problems with their husband, although they did not divorce. The most common problem was that their husband in Indonesia was having affairs while they were working in Hong Kong. One woman specifically admitted that her husband physically abused her before she came to work in Hong Kong. Seven women were mothers. Two of the seven said that their husband was taking care of the children. The other five said that their own parents were caring for the children. Twenty-eight of the women were unmarried. Three of the twenty-eight unmarried women had been engaged to men in Indonesia; however, all three had problems with their fiancé when they were working in Hong Kong and cancelled their engagement. The other twenty-five did not have any concrete plans around marriage yet. Their views on marriage, including the different views held by the unmarried *cewek* and *tomboi*, are discussed in detail in the book.

The *tomboi* and *cewek* in my study used names, whether in Indonesian or English, other than their official names when they socialized with Indonesian migrant women in Hong Kong. The *tomboi* had male names and the *cewek* had female names. To protect their identity, I replaced their names with pseudonyms based on the language and gender of the name that they used in Hong Kong.

Overview of the Book

Chapter 1 establishes the context of the book by providing a wider perspective on both Indonesia and Hong Kong. The first part addresses the changing discourses of home and marriage given the large number of women nationals who have left home to work abroad. The second part discusses the shift in the stance of the Indonesian government toward LGBT individuals and issues. The third part focuses on Hong Kong, particularly on the development of LGBT movements and the emergence of migrant LGBT organizations in the city. Lastly, the changing attitudes of Hong Kong employers toward lesbian migrant workers since the mid-1990s is discussed.

Chapter 2 discusses the formation of gender and sexual subjectivity in the migrant community, particularly the pop dance groups who gather in Victoria Park and Kowloon Park. The first part of the chapter examines the characteristics of the Indonesian migrant community and the gender knowledge produced by their activities. Then, a discussion follows on the sexual ideologies that circulated in the pop dance groups. The discussion includes (1) the formation of a kin world among the pop dance groups, (2) the changing meanings of *tomboi* from its original reference to boyish girls to a sexual identity, (3) how migrant women evaluate biological men, and (4) the meanings of same-sex relationships in the community.

The focus of Chapter 3 is on the intersecting identities of these Indonesian women and how they negotiate an existence subject to the many rules imposed by religion, employers, business owners of karaoke boxes, and landlords of rental rooms. The first part mainly discusses how the women negotiated and reconciled the perceived conflicts between Islam and their same-sex relationships. The second part examines the interactions between Hong Kong people and these Indonesian women in different places, including the home of employer, the karaoke box, and rental rooms. The ways that the Indonesian women responded to gendered expectations in these different spaces is addressed.

The final chapter investigates the sexual subjectivity of these Indonesian women by studying their projected imaginings of home. Since their return to Indonesia is compulsory, I unravel how these women reconciled their future and their desires with family expectations. The first part of the chapter examines their views and emotions toward their actual home in Indonesia. These are significant because they influence the imaginings of home. The second part discusses how the contacts and transactions of travel enable these women to imagine a future home with their female lover. The third part investigates how the imaginaries transform the space of home by *queering* it. The final part turns to those who have decided to return to a heterosexual path in Indonesia. Special attention is placed on understanding how they make sense of their same-sex practices in Hong Kong when they foresee quitting the relationship one day.

1
Discourses of Home, Gender, and Sexuality

Migrant domestic workers are situated in a transnational context in which they have not entirely abandoned their home in Indonesia nor have they fully assimilated into the culture of Hong Kong. Their everyday life, particularly in this study, their gender subjectivities, and their notions of sexuality are tightly linked to the expectations and customs of their parents in Indonesia as well as influenced by the culture and social hierarchy in Hong Kong, where they are marked as foreign maids from a relatively poor country in Southeast Asia. This chapter establishes the context for the specific gender and sexual subjectivities that the Indonesian migrant women in this study found desirable during their stay in Hong Kong.

First, I will briefly provide an introduction to the increase in female labor migration from Indonesia to Hong Kong, which has resulted in a population of around 150,000 Indonesian migrant domestic workers in Hong Kong. Then, I will proceed to examining the changing discourses of home and marriage in Indonesia when such a substantial number of women migrate elsewhere for employment but are expected to return home eventually either to marry or to take care of their elderly parents. This part of the discussion will serve as a background for further investigation of how these women make sense of their migration and experiences in relation to the changing definitions of "happy" family and shifting meanings of marriage.

Second, I will investigate the attitude of the Indonesian government toward lesbian, gay, bisexual, and transgender (LGBT) people at the turn of the century when the political climate changed drastically after the fall of President Suharto in 1998, which marked the beginning of reformation and democracy as well as the rise of Islamic conservatism in Indonesia. I will detail the changes in attitude of the Indonesian government from seeming inclusion to intolerance of LGBT people. The details will contextualize the meanings of same-sex relationships and lesbian identity articulated by the Indonesian migrant women in the chapters that follow.

Hong Kong has striven to present itself as a liberal and democratic city even after the handover to China in 1997. Social movements, including migrant labor activism and LGBT movement, are allowed by the government as long as they are peaceful and do not negatively affect the political structure and economic prosperity. The third part of this chapter will outline the development of LGBT movements in Hong Kong, establishing the background for understanding the visibility of same-sex relationships in Hong Kong.

The final part of this chapter will address the gender expectations that employers impose on their migrant domestic workers. A discussion will follow on the media accounts of lesbianism among migrant domestic workers, serving as crucial background information for understanding how the Indonesian migrant women in this study negotiate their gender appearance and sexual identity with their employer.

Female Labor Migration from Indonesia to Hong Kong

Similar to other developing countries in Asia, Indonesia has relied on nationals to work overseas and remit foreign income back to the country, thereby increasing national earnings, since the early 1990s (Constable 2002; Ehrenreich and Hochschild 2002; Robinson 2009). The authoritarian administration of President Suharto (1965–1998) strategically deployed contradictory and class-specific gender and family ideologies to encourage women from lower-class families to participate in international labor migration while emphasizing that women from middle-class families remain at home to care for their husband and children (Silvey 2006). The Indonesian government also highlighted the economic contributions of migrant workers to the country by labeling them "economic heroes" (*pahlawan devisa*) (Setyawati 2013). Around 750,000 Indonesians leave their country to work overseas every year (Lindquist 2018).

In the mid-1980s, the Indonesian government stipulated that all prospective migrant domestic workers undergo compulsory training in centers operated by recruitment companies to become "skilled" labor before they leave for work abroad (Robinson 2009). This was a national response to incidents in which Indonesian domestic workers were ill treated or even sexually abused by Saudi employers. Instead of addressing these problems by negotiating with the Saudi government, the Indonesian government presented the argument that these women workers were ill treated because they were unskilled and had damaged household appliances or the property of their employer.

The quality of the training programs varies; some recruitment companies are more responsible and provide a mock-up of a Hong Kong apartment, but some just provide lectures and instruction (Anggraeni 2006; Robinson 2009). Sex education is not a mandatory component of the training programs, despite the fact that knowledge of sexual relations is low among these Indonesian migrant workers, as revealed in a survey by Amy Sim. Sim criticized the Indonesian government for leaving the "sexually naïve migrant women open to considerable exploitation" (2010, 43).

The Role of the Family

Family plays a crucial role in facilitating international labor migration. Since the Indonesian government prohibits recruitment agencies from approaching prospective migrant domestic workers directly, agencies now rely on brokers, who are often relatives or neighbors and sometimes even the village head or the wife of the village head, to approach women (Anggraeni 2006; Constable 2014; Lindquist 2009b). Even when a woman decides to work overseas, the broker is required to obtain written consent from either her father or husband before she can travel to the training center in the city. Given that the broker is also a part of this woman's community, it is in the best interest of the broker to gain the trust of her father or husband, who would then be more willing to let the woman leave home for work (Palmer 2010). Besides, the broker also gives cash to the woman's family in advance to encourage them to allow their daughter or wife to work overseas (Lindquist 2009b; Palmer 2010).

Younger sisters may also follow an elder sister who is already working in Hong Kong. In a study by Anggraeni (2006), the parents of one such young woman indicated that they were less worried about allowing their younger daughter to work overseas since their older daughter was already sending money back home from Hong Kong regularly. The younger daughter was also more confident with her older sister in the same city. A family with one daughter already working overseas is more likely to send other daughters abroad, especially when the first daughter has done well.

Although family plays a crucial role in facilitating labor migration, Indonesian law (Law No. 39/2004) does not grant family members any legal right to information about the overseas job or the right to communicate with a daughter or wife working overseas. The International Organization for Migration (2010) reported that many families actually lose contact with their daughter or wife after she leaves Indonesia.

The Indonesian Discourse of Home

Indonesian society regards marriage and motherhood the primary role of women when they reach adulthood. However, the long years that women are away from their families for overseas employment have complicated women's roles. Married women can justify their absence from home by redefining the meaning and practice of motherhood. Rachel Silvey noted that Indonesian women who went to Saudi Arabia as domestic workers have redefined motherhood by valuing the monetary outcome of working overseas over the care that a mother is supposed to directly give to her children. As noted by a mother informant in her study, "My kids needed the money more than they needed me" (2006, 30). This view was also reflected in villagers' understanding of the purpose of migration. The villagers perceived migration as a woman's duty to fulfill the needs of the family first and foremost, especially the needs of children.

As is the case with their married counterparts, unmarried women share the goal of meeting the "needs of the family," for example, satisfying the material needs of their parents by building a new brick house for the family, rather than by living with and taking care of their aged parents (Anggraeni 2006; Lan 2006). Dewi Anggraeni (2006) interviewed a single woman who said that while it is good to live close to her parents, she still decided to work overseas as her income would help to improve their life, which she considered the most important factor.

The family power dynamic has also changed in subtle ways. Women who left home and gained work experience in the city indicated that their parents and family members respected them more than before. For example, one of the informants said that her father consulted with her whether he should sell the rice field despite her married brother having already advised him to sell the property. In the past, the voices of single women were not taken into consideration when parents had to make important decisions (Situmorang 2011). The status of single women in the family has therefore improved, given their increasing financial power as well as their wider exposure to cities and other countries.

Nevertheless, despite the emphasis in narratives of migrant women, including both married and unmarried women, on the financial incentives of working abroad, Pei-Chia Lan (2006) noted that they do not originate from the poorest areas of the country but the more developed regions. Her observation reminds us that the needs of a family are indeed shaped by materialism; the decision to migrate is affected by the social norms of achievement and adventure.

The discourse of home has also come to be represented in more materialistic terms. As noted by Silvey (2006), family has become an arena for women and their families to process their own desires for commodities and newly painted houses in the post-Suharto era. Both economic development and the soap operas that circulate images of modern houses in the city contribute to the new meanings of a happy family (Anggraeni 2006). Family ideology has changed as consumer goods and materialistic satisfaction are now the basic components of a "happy" family. Shaped by the new discourse of home, these women identify with the obligation to fulfill the family's material needs by working overseas, even though they are aware that they might face misfortune and pain in the process of migration (Silvey 2006).

Marriage

In the rural areas of Indonesia, overseas employment has strong connotations of modernity because the opportunity to work abroad allows the person to learn things and reach people beyond the village (Lindquist 2009b; Warouw 2008). Particularly for secondary school graduates in rural areas,[1] overseas employment is a sound work opportunity because they do not wish to work in the rice fields as their parents have (Situmorang 2011) but their education level and limited personal networks are far below what is needed to find a decent job in the city. As noted by Lan (2006), about 23 percent of the Indonesian domestic workers in her study were factory workers, and 17 percent were salesclerks or waitresses before they went to Taiwan. Jobs in the city are very limited for women without a tertiary education. Besides, the pay in the cities of Indonesia is far less than the income from overseas employment because of the economic disparity between Indonesia and the receiving countries of overseas workers (Anggraeni 2006).

While these women have identified overseas employment as a means of securing a desirable job as well as a bridge to modernity, they are also aware that migrant domestic workers are regularly exposed to a variety of dangers (Lan 2006, 128). Stories of Indonesian workers assaulted by their overseas employer are widely circulated in Indonesia, such as the case of Erwiana Sulistyaningsih, who was abused by her Hong Kong employer in 2014, which received international attention.

Moreover, the issue of the sexual reputation of migrant domestic workers has drawn much media and social attention in Indonesia (Constable 2014; Silvey 2006). As noted by Carol Chan (2016), when villagers heard that a particular woman was able to remit a surprisingly large amount of money to her parents every month, rumors spread in the village that she was a sex worker. The migrant workers themselves are also aware of the bad reputation that goes along with working abroad, which means that Indonesian women who go to Hong Kong are believed to lack sexual morality (Mathews 2011).

While the issue of sexual reputation might jeopardize marriageability in the village, it does not stop these women from leaving home. Instead, they reconcile the issue of sexual reputation by anticipating greater autonomy in choosing their future marriage partner. In a study of Indonesian migrant women in Lombok, a tourist area in Indonesia where sex tourism is well known, an unmarried woman told Linda Rae Bennett (2008) that she had no regrets about taking a job there although her sexual reputation would be subject to scrutiny in her hometown.

---

1. Indonesia has a nine-year mandatory education system. Women who have a secondary level of education reached 75 percent in Indonesia in 2014 (UNICEF 2016). According to a survey conducted by the Asian Migrant Centre in 2007, 88 percent of the Indonesian domestic workers in Hong Kong have a secondary education (AMC, IMWU, and KOTKIHO 2007).

She said that her spousal ideals have also changed. She would like to marry a man who is not from a village but someone who has been exposed to urban life with similar work experience and therefore is less likely to judge her sexual reputation. The notions of sexual reputation and spousal ideals become malleable in the process of overseas employment when women possess greater autonomy in making life choices.

Single women also perceive overseas employment as a feasible way to defer arranged marriages at a young age. Pei-Chia Lan (2006) interviewed a single woman from West Java who said that at twenty years old, she was betrothed to a farmer. She instead went to work in Saudi Arabia despite her parents' objection. She mentioned to Lan that she had seen many women who had married when they were not even twenty years old and ended up divorcing the man.

For married women, overseas employment is more like a double-edged sword. On the one hand, working overseas is a decision the couple makes together to secure a better future for themselves and their children. On the other hand, many husbands start affairs with other women during their absence (Borch 2008). As Rachel Silvey (2006) stated, there is a common view among Indonesian migrant women that divorce is inevitable after a long separation because the sexual needs of the husband are unmet. The narratives of the migrant women contribute to normalizing the husband's infidelity as well as the instability of marriage when the women are absent from home for years at a time.

Divorced women usually face discrimination in their communities because they are perceived as failed women. Additionally, there is a lack of institutional support for single mothers in Indonesian societies. The single mothers in the study by Constable on migrant domestic workers in Hong Kong reported that they had significant difficulty in obtaining a birth certificate for their newborn after returning to Indonesia. The mothers said that the Indonesian officials refused to issue a birth certificate unless they could produce a marriage certificate (2014, 229).

Despite the discrimination and prejudice against single mothers, the social conditions that single mothers face vary depending on the status of the father of the baby and the financial ability of the woman. As noted by Constable (2014), a single mother would still be accepted and respected by her community if (1) the father is an Indonesian; (2) she has married the father of her baby, and the marriage is recognized by her community; and most importantly, (3) the woman is able to financially support herself and her children. On the contrary, shame, discrimination, and social exclusion are expected if the children are born out of wedlock during her stay in a foreign country (which implies that the father is unknown) and, worse, the woman cannot make a living in Indonesia.

Indonesian society generally looks down on single mothers who have children out of wedlock. Seemingly, men do not want to marry this kind of woman. However, a single mother with a child born out of wedlock in the study by Constable (2014) was able to marry an Indonesian man after returning from Hong Kong. Her friends, who were also migrant domestic workers in Hong Kong, told Constable that there are Indonesian men who do not mind marrying a single mother if they think that she would go abroad to work and send him money. This story reveals that the marriageability of single mothers with children born out of wedlock is in fact intertwined with their perceived financial ability, especially those who work overseas. An ideal marriage in which the man is the breadwinner and the woman is a virgin is severely contested.

Female Same-Sex Intimacy and Lesbianism in Indonesia

Intimate behaviors between two young unmarried women, such as holding hands when walking, sleeping together, and cuddling, are not uncommon in Indonesia and other Southeast Asian regions (Blackwood 2010; Sinnott 2004). People generally perceive intimacy between women as a form of sisterhood or close friendship (*sahabat*). In Indonesia, homosocial relationships are highly encouraged because making friends with men might create gossip and elicit unwanted attention (Situmorang 2011). Previous studies have shown that women who are sexually attracted to other women are able to use sisterhood as a camouflage; these women develop same-sex relationships without drawing much attention from their families and neighbors (Blackwood 2010; Wieringa 2007). Some couples are even able to set up a household as long as they do not force their parents and neighbors to acknowledge their same-sex relationship.

It is noteworthy that the Indonesian society does not support lesbianism even though intimacy between two women is socially acceptable. The notion that "lesbianism is an illness and deviance" became popular in Indonesia when print media began to report about lesbians in the 1990s. Newspaper columnists in mainstream newspapers depicted lesbians as prostitutes, drug abusers, or criminals (Blackwood 2010). A national Indonesian newspaper, *Koran Tempo*, featured a full-page article titled "Lesbianism from a Psychiatric View" ("Lesbian dalam Pandangan Psikiatrik"), dated June 14, 2012. The article claimed that lesbianism is a sexual disorder (*gangguan seksual*) and should be treated by psychiatrists. It concludes:

> Considering that lesbianism is a sexual disorder and has become more obvious, we should start prevention work and enact strong regulations to reduce the number and the prevalence of lesbianism. . . . A psychiatric approach can cure lesbians. [Mengingat lesbian adalah gangguan seksual yang makin marak, sebaiknya kita segera melakukan pencegahan dan pengelolaan yang adekuat untuk menekan angka insidensi dan prevalensinya. . . . Pendekatan psikiatrik dapat meembantu penyembuhan lesbian.] (Soewadi 2012)

Ignoring the fact that the American Psychiatric Association has removed homosexuality entirely from the *Diagnostic and Statistical Manual of Mental Disorders* in 1986 (Herek 2012), the article claimed that lesbianism is a sexual disorder and urged lesbians to seek help from psychiatrists. Sadly, the article did not provide any scientific evidence to support the claim.

Organizations that focus on the rights of lesbians, bisexual, and transgender people in the capital city of Indonesia have emerged since the late 1990s. The first lesbian organization was Swara Srikandi (The Voice of Srikandi), which started its work on the internet in 2000. At the beginning, Swara Srikandi maintained a low profile because its members did not want to be identified as lesbians because of the negative connotations. In 2002, they began to work anonymously with the media with the aim of promoting a positive image of Indonesian lesbians. Another lesbian group is Sector 15, which was formed in 1998 within the Indonesian Women's Coalition (Koalisi Perempuan Indonesia) (Blackwood 2007). Sector 15, which serves sexual minorities, includes lesbians and bisexual and transgender people among its members. In 2005, the Ardhanary Institute (AI) was established in Jakarta. Its founding leader was a member of Sector 15. The work of the AI includes both advocacy for sexual rights and training on reproductive health and self-acceptance for lesbians and bisexual and transgender people (Khanis 2013). Members of the AI celebrated the 2012 International Day against Homophobia in a public area of Jakarta with their faces painted in masquerade masks (Walton 2013). In 2006, the Women's Rainbow Institute (Institut Pelangi Perempuan, IPP) was established and served Indonesian lesbians in Jakarta. The IPP organized monthly gatherings, such as film screenings and discussion groups related to lesbian issues. The IPP also published an online magazine and managed an online mailing list to exchange information among its lesbian members. The group endeavors to network lesbians through different means. But both AI and IPP maintain a low profile in the neighborhood. I visited the two groups through a friend's network in 2007. The two offices were located in ordinary neighborhoods. There was no signage of their organization or a rainbow flag outside their offices. The leaders of AI and IPP said that outsiders and neighbors do not know that they are lesbian organizations.

Intolerant Attitudes of the Government toward Lesbians and LGBT Issues

There is no explicit law against consensual homosexual acts between adults in Indonesia (Hutton 2017). This might create the impression that the Indonesian government tolerates homosexuality, but this is only a misconception. The following will address how both the globalization of LGBT rights and the political transformation of Indonesia have led the Indonesian government to suppress homosexuality in a more explicit way.

As noted by Boellstorff (2004a) in his earlier work, the assumed tolerance of homosexuality by the Indonesian government exists only because LGBT Indonesians do not publicly proclaim their social and sexual rights. The Indonesian government began to demonstrate intolerance toward homosexuality when LGBT groups in Indonesia emerged to claim equal rights and international organizations pressed for same-sex marriage in the mid-1990s, forcing a new response from the Indonesian government. In 1994, the Indonesian minister of population declared at the International Conference on Population and Development that Indonesia would not support same-sex marriage (Blackwood 2010). In the same year, the minister for women's affairs stated that "lesbianism is not part of Indonesian culture or state ideology" (Murray 1999, 142). Homosexuality was constructed by the government as a foreign concept imported from the West as a result of globalization (Wieringa 2015).

In 1999, Abdurrahman Wahid, a Muslim leader, became the president of Indonesia after Suharto stepped down in 1998. The change of presidency contributed to the spread of Islamic conservatism, which began to influence state ideology and attempted to regulate public morality at the national level. For example, there was a call for the implementation of Sharia law (Islamic law) in Indonesia's legal codes (Brenner 2011). The pornography law was passed in 2008 to regulate the sexual morality of the country. The law defines "deviant sexual acts" to include male homosexual, lesbian, oral, and anal sex, as well as sex with animals and corpses. The Indonesian police raided two hotel rooms in Surabaya and arrested fourteen gay men on charges of violating the pornography law in 2017 (Human Rights Watch 2017a). After the raid in Surabaya, the police in Jakarta raided a gym and sauna and arrested 141 men for holding a "gay sex party" on charges of violating the same law (*Daily Mail Online* 2017).

There has been an uptick in violence against homosexuality. In 2000, 150 members of an Islamic youth organization called the Ka'bah Youth Movement burst into a celebration hosted by gay and transgender groups in observance of National Health Day in Kaliurang, Central Java. The attackers assaulted those who were present with knives, machetes, and clubs. At least twenty-five were injured and bloodied (Boellstorff 2004a). In 2003, death threats were made to lesbian and gay groups on television (Wieringa 2007). In 2010, the regional Asian conference in Surabaya was forced to cancel because of attacks started by hardline Islamic groups (Boellstorff 2016). The Indonesian government did little to stop the Islamic groups. LGBT citizens are not protected by the government when they face violence.

Worse was to follow. In 2016, the government became actively involved in curbing homosexuality. Boellstorff (2016) argued that the change was influenced not only by the hardline Islamic groups but also by the national awareness of the advances of LGBT rights that might help create a future in which Indonesia would recognize citizens who proclaim a homosexual identity. This moral panic led the government to curb homosexuality more proactively and to increase its intolerance of LGBT issues. The government took the stance that LGBT issues threaten the public morality of Indonesia.

The government has already taken action and implemented cultural, medical, and educational policies against LGBT people (Boellstorff 2016; Wieringa 2017). In terms of cultural policy, the Indonesian Broadcasting Commission banned male effeminacy from all television shows (*Jakarta Post* 2016c). The Communications and Information Ministry announced that it would draft a bill to ban websites that "promote LGBT propaganda" (*Jakarta Post* 2016a). In the medical sector, the Indonesian Psychiatrists Association identified LGBT people as having mental disorders (*Jakarta Post* 2016b). Despite the protest of psychiatric bodies around the world, the Indonesian association has no intention of reversing its decision. In the education sector, the minister of research, technology, and higher education said that LGBT individuals should be barred from university campuses (*Jakarta Post* 2016d).

Same-sex couples now living together may not be as safe as before. Twelve Indonesian women were suspected to be lesbians, and police raided their homes in a village of West Java Province after receiving complaints from Islamic groups and religious leaders in 2017. According to the report, the women were suspected to be lesbians because "some have short hair, acting as the males. Some have long hair, acting as the females" (Human Rights Watch 2017b). Claiming that their presence created a public disturbance in the area, the police forced the women to leave the village within three days.

Anti-LGBT sentiment continued to rise as the 2019 Indonesian presidential election campaign started. The supporters of Prabowo Subianto, the opponent of Joko Widodo, spread rumors that legalization of LGBT people will follow if Widodo is reelected (Merigo 2019). Joko Widodo then posted a message "Stop Hoax" on his Twitter account to dismiss the rumors. This Twitter message revealed that Widodo had no plan to speak up for LGBT people although he had promised to improve the human rights conditions of Indonesia when he ran in the 2014 presidential election (*Straits Times* 2019a). For the 2019 election, Widodo selected Ma'ruf Amin, a top Islamic cleric, as his vice presidential running mate to show his embrace of Islamic values (Allard and Asmarini 2018). Amin had been the chairman of Indonesia's Ulama Council and helped to draft fatwas (religious edicts) to punish same-sex acts and called for the criminalization of LGBT activities (Human Rights Watch 2018). Widodo and Amin won the 2019 election (BBC 2019).

Various national parties have prepared legislation and called for the criminalization of LGBT people in Indonesia. In September 2019, serious riots broke out in Jakarta in response to the proposal of penal code changes, which would criminalize consensual sex outside marriage (*Straits Times* 2019b). Since same-sex couples cannot get married in Indonesia, they would violate the penal code if they are found to be engaging in sexual activity or living together. Widodo did not call for a delay in passing the revisions until severe riots broke out.

LGBT Movements in Hong Kong

Homosexuality was decriminalized in Hong Kong in 1991 (Refworld 2008). This section will discuss (1) the development of LGBT movements after decriminalization, (2) the backlash from Christian groups, (3) the public attitude toward LGBT people, and (4) the emergence of lesbian organizations established by Filipino and Indonesian migrant domestic workers.

Inherited from British colonial governance, Hong Kong has a tradition of liberalism that tolerates rallies and protests (Wee and Sim 2005). After its handover to China under the policy of "One Country, Two Systems" in 1997, the Hong Kong government strived to maintain its status as Asia's world city. The government continued the policy of tolerating peaceful rallies and protests that do not threaten the wider economic interests of Hong Kong (Constable 2011). In 2005, the first march for the International Day against Homophobia was held by local LGBT groups. In 2008, the first Hong Kong Pride Parade was held. The parade is now an annual event that starts in Causeway Bay, one of the busiest areas in Hong Kong. The parade attracts both locals and tourists from Taiwan, mainland China, Southeast Asia, and Euro-America. The organizers recorded a gradual increase in the number of participants from 1,000 in 2008 to 12,000 in 2018 (*HK01* 2018; Hong Kong Pride Parade 2018). In addition, three public figures, Denise Ho (a female pop singer), Anthony Wong (a male pop singer), and Raymond Chan Chi-chuen (a male legislative councilor), publicly came out in 2012 and later established a new group for LGBT rights called Big Love Alliance (Kong, Lau, and Li 2015). In 2013, York Chow, the government-appointed chairperson of the Equal Opportunities Commission (EOC), attended the parade. He was the first EOC chairperson to join the parade and publicly express his support for sexual minorities (Ngo 2016).

The Hong Kong government also took part in promoting equal opportunity for people of different sexual orientations. In 2005, the Gender Identity and Sexual Orientation Unit was established under the Constitutional and Mainland Affairs Bureau. The unit maintains a hotline for complaints on issues related to sexual orientation and gender identity. It has also established the Code of Practice against Discrimination in Employment on the Ground of Sexual Orientation, although the code is not an ordinance and employers are not bound by any legal obligation to follow it. The government also set up the Equal Opportunity (Sexual Orientation) Funding Scheme in the same year to provide funding support to community projects that aim to promote equal opportunities for people of different sexual orientations and transgender people. In 2013, the Constitutional and Mainland Affairs Bureau launched its first-ever television promotion in the form of a thirty-second commercial that promoted equal opportunities for sexual minorities (Government of the Hong Kong Special Administrative Region 2005). The message of eliminating discrimination against people of different sexual orientations and transgender people is clearly articulated in this television clip.

As China has signed the United Nations (UN) Treaty on Human Rights, the human rights conditions in Hong Kong are monitored by the UN. The UN Committee on Economic, Social, and Cultural Rights urged the Hong Kong government to prohibit discrimination based on sexual orientation in 2001 and 2005 (United Nations Committee on Economic, Social and Cultural Rights 2001, 2005). Up until 2019, when I was revising this chapter, Hong Kong still did not have any laws that prohibit discrimination based on sexual orientation. Nevertheless, gay and lesbian individuals are applying for judicial reviews to challenge Hong Kong laws that they found discriminatory. In 2004, a judicial review was filed to challenge Hong Kong laws that prohibited consensual male homosexual sex under the age of twenty-one, while the age of consent for heterosexual sex is sixteen. The court ruled that the laws were unconstitutional and undermined human rights under the city's Bill of Rights and the Basic Law (*South China Morning Post* 2005). This is a landmark court case that has changed the impact of the law on LGBT people—once a tool to suppress the private lives of LGBT people, the judicial system has become a new arena for LGBT people to pursue their rights (Cho, Kam, and Lai 2018). More judicial reviews concerning the rights of LGBT people came after this landmark case. For instance, a judicial review was filed in 2014 by a British woman who had entered into a civil partnership with her same-sex partner in the UK. When her partner relocated to work in Hong Kong, her application for a dependent visa was denied. She then filed a judicial review to challenge the immigration policy that granted dependent visas only to married heterosexual couples. After a three-year legal battle, the highest court ruled against the Immigration Department and required it to grant spousal visas to same-sex couples (Lau 2018).

There is backlash against LGBT rights from Christian groups. When the government launched a poll to study public attitudes toward nonheterosexual people in 2005, many Christian groups were afraid that the government would establish a sexual orientation discrimination ordinance. Christian groups then launched a series of newspaper advertisements that claimed that sexual promiscuity and AIDS were rampant among homosexuals. They also lobbied politicians about the social problems that would be created if a sexual orientation discrimination ordinance were established (Kong Lau, and Li 2015). They argued that the monogamous heterosexual nuclear family is the pillar of social order and public morality (Wong 2013).

Despite the backlash from Christian groups, public attitudes toward homosexuality and, broadly, people of different sexual orientations and gender identities have greatly improved, as shown in a poll commissioned by the Equal

Opportunities Commission and conducted by the Gender Research Centre of the Chinese University of Hong Kong in 2016. At least three points in the report (Suen et al. 2016) are worth noting. First, it found that 55.7 percent of the public "somewhat/completely" agreed that there should be legal protection against discrimination on the grounds of sexual orientation, gender identity, and intersex status. This is a significant increase when compared to a poll conducted ten years ago, in which only 28.7 percent of the public agreed that there should be legal protection. Second, 91.8 percent of the respondents between eighteen to twenty-four years old were supportive of legislation against discrimination on the grounds of sexual orientation, gender identity, and intersex status. This shows that Hong Kong society is becoming more liberal toward LGBT people. Third, there is a diverse range of views among the respondents with religious beliefs, in which 48.9 percent agree that there should be legal protection against discrimination on the grounds of sexual orientation, gender identity, and intersex status. This indicates that the backlash from the Christian groups does not reflect or represent the diverse views of respondents with religious beliefs.

Among the Chinese-dominated LGBT movements,[2] a few lesbian organizations have been formed by migrant domestic workers since 2006. Filguys Association Hong Kong was founded by Marrz Balaoro, a Filipino migrant domestic worker in Hong Kong. It started with 21 members and now exceeds 400, with members from Australia, Canada, and the United States (*HK01* 2016; *Time Out Hong Kong* 2012). From 2007 to 2012, Filguys joined the march for the International Day against Homophobia hosted by Hong Kong LGBT groups. Filguys held a clear vision of fighting discrimination and homophobia as well as for the rights and welfare of Filipino migrant workers. The association held a street forum on lesbian rights on Chater Road, Central, on June 17, 2012. In addition to other Filipino workers, unexpectedly two or three South Asian men who were selling items to the Filipinos also listened to the forum. While I was giving a speech about myself as a lesbian who supported the rights of migrant lesbians, a South Asian man, who was presumably offended, shouted at me. He did not escalate to violence toward me or the forum host but stared at us angrily. Chater Road is an ideal place for holding events on lesbian rights because the location is a hub of Filipino workers on Sundays and its open area also enables Filguys Association Hong Kong to promote its activities to other Filipino workers. However, my personal experience reflects Filguys' vulnerability of because passers-by who have no tolerance for lesbians can easily interrupt the events with verbal violence.

Other lesbian organizations formed by the Filipino migrant workers included the Filipino Lesbian Organization and Filguys Association Gabriela Hong Kong (a different group established by a former member of Filguys Association Hong

---

2. The Chinese population comprises over 90 percent of the people in the city of Hong Kong.

Kong). These two lesbian groups held the first-ever Migrants Pride March in 2015 with support from Gabriela, a Filipino grassroots women's organization, and its Hong Kong chapter, Gabriela Hong Kong. The organizing committee of the Migrants Pride March, recognizing importance of allying with other migrant worker organizations as well as connecting with Hong Kong activist groups, invited the Asian Migrants Coordinating Body to be one of the organizing parties in 2016. Several Hong Kong activist groups, such as the Association for the Advancement of Feminism and Left 21 (a left-wing platform for social equality and progress), also came to support the event (F. Y. Lai 2018a).

In addition to joining the Hong Kong Pride Parade, they also organize their own pride events. The organizer explained that she has attended the Hong Kong Pride Parade since 2012; however, she found it difficult to mobilize other migrant workers to take part because the Hong Kong Pride Parade is held on a Saturday every year, which is not a day off for most migrant domestic workers. Therefore, she decided to hold a pride march for migrants on a Sunday in Central (a hub of Filipino domestic workers on Sundays), where she could easily attract Filipino workers to attend (*WKNews* 2015). Besides, they could deliver their message more effectively using their own language in the march. Shiela Tebia, the chairperson of Gabriela Hong Kong, acknowledged that one of the goals of the Migrants Pride March is to educate Filipino lesbians that they have the right to live as lesbians both in Hong Kong and even after they return home to the Philippines (F. Y. Lai 2018a). She emphasized that it is crucial to increase Filipino workers' confidence in their lesbian identity, so that they would not succumb to social and familial pressure in the Philippines to return to a heterosexual identity.

Within the Indonesian migrant community, a lesbian organization called Dunia Kita (Our World), was founded in 2013 by a lesbian couple who are both domestic workers in Hong Kong. It began with about twenty members who are all Indonesian migrant domestic workers. The president of Dunia Kita contacted me via Facebook after a referral from one of the Indonesian women in this study. I was invited to act as a consultant for Dunia Kita, helping to write proposals for external funding. Dunia Kita educated members about human rights, particularly LGBT rights, and organized gatherings for those who are in same-sex relationships to share their struggles with family and religion. The organization also provided media interviews that addressed discrimination against lesbian domestic workers by prejudiced Hong Kong employers. However, the president of Dunia Kita decided to cease operation in 2014 because of unresolved conflicts among its members over whether to maintain a high profile in the face of increasing media reports about the group and migrant lesbians.

Indonesian Magazine Bans Lesbianism in Hong Kong

The lesbian activities of migrant workers in Hong Kong do not go unnoticed in Indonesia. A magazine published by an editorial team in Gresik, a city near Surabaya, Indonesia, called *Pandu: Menuju BMI Mandiri & Berprestasi* (Guide: Indonesian migrant workers toward independence and achievement) positions itself as a guide for Indonesian migrant women by emphasizing Indonesian Islamic values. The price of each copy is HKD 10 (approx. USD 1.30).

The magazine features pictures of men and women in Islamic clothing—men wear an Islamic hat and women wear a *jilbab* (Islamic headscarf). In the November 2010 edition, the cover story was "Sisi Gelap Kebebasan" (The dark side of freedom). The cover pictured three Indonesian women posed as though they were in a romantic triangle: one *tomboi*-like woman held by another woman; another *tomboi*-like woman holds that woman's arm. The title and picture suggest that lesbian relationships are the dark side of freedom. The first article in the magazine addressed the dark side of freedom, including promiscuity, pregnancy outside wedlock, abortion, HIV/AIDS, lesbianism, frequenting discos, and alcohol and drug use. The follow-up article on lesbianism was titled "Cinta Sejenis yang Mengakibatkan Aku Radang Usus" (Same-sex love that caused me enteritis). The article is about a former lesbian who described her painful experience in a lesbian relationship: she suffered from enteritis for three months, and her same-sex lover met a handsome *tomboi* and did not go with her to the medical clinic for treatment. In the last paragraph, she wrote:

> After I was awakened, I felt grateful. Allah loves me and gave me pain that was caused by same-sex love. I would not do it anymore. [Setelah aku terbangun, aku merasa bersyukur. Allah menyayangiku, dengan memberi rasa sakit yang tak terperi akibat cinta sejenis. Aku takkan mengulanginya.] (Arum 2010, 9)

The magazine article constructs Hong Kong as an overly free society that causes some Indonesian migrant women to leave Allah and become lesbians or fallen women. The magazine does not directly blame Indonesian women who become lesbians but marks them as victims of globalization. According to the magazine, migrant women become lesbians because they are stressed out in Hong Kong; the problem of lesbianism would be solved if they prayed and listened to Allah. Another key message delivered by the magazine is that lesbianism is a sin in Islam; Allah does not accept lesbians and will punish them. As the article suggests, Allah used the pain of enteritis to punish a lesbian for her homosexual behavior.

Hong Kong Employers

The number of migrant domestic workers in Hong Kong has increased from a few hundred in the 1970s to more than 369,000 as of December 2017 (Census and Statistics Department, the Government of the Hong Kong Special Administrative Region 2018a). There are approximately 160,000 Indonesian women and 197,000 Filipino women among the 369,000 migrant domestic workers. On average, one out of seven households in Hong Kong has employed at least one migrant domestic worker (Census and Statistics Department, the Government of the Hong Kong Special Administrative Region 2018b). From the 1980s onward, full-time housewives became less common in Hong Kong because educated women, who were previously unemployed, began to join the labor market because of expanding employment opportunities in the service, administrative, and clerical sectors (Constable 2000). Demand for full-time, live-in domestic workers to provide childcare, cooking, cleaning, and care of the elderly has grown. However, local women generally consider domestic work degrading. The introduction of migrant domestic workers was seen an ideal solution for both the Hong Kong government and dual-career families.

Employer control over the migrant worker's body and sexuality is not a new issue. In her book published two decades ago, Constable (1997) already noted how Hong Kong employers disciplined the body and sexuality of their migrant domestic workers by establishing household rules, such as forbidding workers to wear sleeveless clothes and setting a curfew on their days off. Constable also noted employers' underlying assumption that their migrant domestic workers were a sexual threat. Constable argued that capitalism and sexuality were intrinsically linked in the discourses of the nineteenth-century Industrial Revolution, in which lower-class women left their families to work for wages. Lower-class women are constructed as dangerous and filthy because they are nurtured in a poorly articulated social system and may approach men to make money. Migrant domestic workers in Hong Kong are subject to this discourse and positioned as dangerous because they originate from relatively poor countries and, more importantly, because they live under the same roof as their employer. Therefore, female employers defeminize their live-in workers to minimize the sexual threat, as these workers are usually younger than they.

Migrant domestic workers wearing men's clothing and short hair went unnoticed and were interpreted as heterosexually neutral until the media began to report lesbianism among migrant workers with a television documentary in 1996 (Constable 2000). Homophobia against masculine-looking domestic workers started to emerge in 1996 when the documentary quoted a Filipino worker who estimated that a quarter of all Filipino domestic workers were lesbians. Hong Kong employers began to express concern and wrote letters to the local newspapers about the problem of lesbianism among migrant domestic workers. Approximately a decade later, Hong Kong society appears to hold a rather open attitude toward masculine-looking migrant workers. Amy Sim noted the change in employer attitudes in her research on Indonesian migrant workers conducted from 2002 to 2005. Sim noted that the number of openly lesbian Indonesian migrant workers who were accepted by their employer was increasing. On Sundays, the masculine-identifying lesbians were easily identified by their baggy pants, oversized tees, and baseball caps. Sim argued that the dress code was a shared symbol of for Indonesian lesbians to mark their sexual preference for women (Sim 2010).

The changing social attitude toward migrant lesbians is also reflected in media accounts in Hong Kong. On November 9, 2013, *Apple Daily*, a mainstream Hong Kong Chinese newspaper, interviewed the president of Dunia Kita. It was a side story of the Hong Kong Pride Parade, which took place on that day. The president said that the employers of some of their members tell them that they are not allowed to be involved in same-sex relationships. One member was scolded and insulted by her employer when her same-sex relationship was revealed. The president said that there are employers who confuse pedophilia with lesbianism. She also said that they hope employers would understand that there is no relationship between sexual orientation and work performance.

For two consecutive days before Valentine's Day in 2014, *Apple Daily* ran stories on an Indonesian lesbian couple and one of their employer. It was a special feature for the holiday. The couple allowed the reporter to take their picture. Both women said that their employer had already accepted their sexual orientation. One employer, Ms. Mak, was also interviewed. Ms. Mak admired her domestic worker very much and said, "She is very attentive to her work. . . . [W]hen my colleagues saw her, they asked whether she is a boy or girl, and why is she so masculine. I don't think her gender appearance matters. I don't mind whether her partner is a man or woman. I can tell that the couple respect each other" (*Apple Daily* 2014b).

On January 2, 2014, the *House News*,[3] a *Huffington Post*–like Hong Kong Chinese online news platform, republished a feature story on a lesbian couple in Hong Kong, originally written by a Hong Kong Chinese lesbian group called Lime. The article showed two wedding pictures of the couple, in which one wore a man's wedding suit and the other one wore a wedding gown. The couple said that their employer accepted their same-sex relationship. The author ended the article with a supportive comment, which I translated from Chinese into English: "Perhaps they are not the most tough people; they face pressures of all sorts,

---

3. House News ceased operation on July 24, 2014. One of the cofounders, Tony Choi, explained the decision was made because of the increasing political pressure from mainland China. Choi's announcement in Chinese: https://web.archive.org/web/20140726163736/http://thehousenews.com/.

they give courage to their loved ones. Hope they would be together for the rest of their lives" (*House News* 2014).

On January 17, 2012, *Time Out Hong Kong*, a branch of the international consumer magazine *Time Out*, interviewed the founder of Filguys Association Hong Kong on the difficulties that lesbian domestic workers face and included a picture of the founder in the article. The founder said in the interview that she was very lucky because her employer had already accepted her sexual orientation. She also mentioned that there are employers who might fear that lesbian domestic workers would influence their children with ideas on homosexuality. The reporter ended the article with a supportive statement: "Filguys is working hard to create a safe place for their members" (*Time Out Hong Kong* 2012).

The above media accounts show a liberal attitude toward lesbian relationships of migrant domestic workers. The message that sexual orientation does not affect work or integrity, as well as that migrant lesbians are entitled to equal employment opportunities, was clearly articulated in media reports. Second, the lesbians interviewed were depicted as brave because they chose to come out to their employer. Their image of bravery is reinforced by the publication of full-face pictures alongside the articles. Third, a division between "good employers" and "bad employers" was established by these media accounts. "Good employers" are like Ms. Mak and respect the sexual rights of their domestic workers. In contrast, "bad employers" are those who misunderstand lesbianism as pedophilia or insult their workers because of their sexual orientation.

Summary

This chapter has provided the contexts of both Indonesian and Hong Kong societies for understanding the rest of the book, particularly how Indonesian women make sense of their sexuality and find same-sex relationships desirable during their stay in Hong Kong. But I need to clarify that I have no intention of saying that Hong Kong is a better place than Indonesia when I describe the LGBT movement in Hong Kong and the intolerant atmosphere against LGBT issues in Indonesia. While the city of Hong Kong is relatively liberal and can accommodate a Pride Parade and judicial reviews that challenge discriminatory laws against homosexuality, misconceptions about and discrimination against LGBT people persists in the city. The emergence of migrant lesbian organizations and media accounts both prove that there is discrimination against migrant workers who are having same-sex relationships. Migrant lesbian organizations are founded not because a place is safe for them; instead, groups form there to help and empower those who are discriminated against or even fired because of their same-sex relationship.

Public attitudes toward LGBT people tend to be accepting, as shown in the study of Amy Sim (2010) and Suen et al. (2016). Both serve as a backdrop for understanding how Indonesian migrant women can make room for their intimate behaviors and same-sex relationships in the city. Although the fieldwork was conducted a few years earlier (from 2010 to 2012), the EOC report still shows the improving social atmosphere for LGBT people when compared to the poll conducted in 2006.

Anti-LGBT sentiment in Indonesia is intensifying. The raid on suspected lesbians shows that sisterhood as camouflage for two women in a same-sex relationship does not always work. In addition, it is noteworthy that the Indonesian government and political parties work with Islamic leaders and organizations to gain people's trust and votes in elections. The LGBT community struggles to survive in Indonesia subject to the pressure from both the government and religious groups. The social context of Indonesia helps to contextualize the stories of the Indonesian women in the following chapters, especially how they think about their same-sex relationship, which is considered a sin in Islam; how they reconcile the assumed conflicts between Islam and lesbian behavior; and whether they want to continue the relationship after returning to Indonesia.

Millions of Indonesian women have left to work overseas. Material satisfaction is becoming more important when Indonesian people come to think about what constitutes a happy family and dutiful womanhood. Although Indonesian society still perceives women working overseas as morally loose and questions their sexual purity, unmarried women are aware of their earning potential as an asset on the marriage market in Indonesia. Some returned migrant women divorce their husband in Indonesia; some even come back with children born out of wedlock. Materialism and the assumed financial security of returned migrant women have lessened the stigma imposed on their nonnormative status and behaviors. The changing notion of womanhood is crucial for understanding how the Indonesian women in this study think about their future as well as their imaginings of home.

2
Gender and Sexuality in the Migrant Community

I first approached the Indonesian migrant community for this research project in 2010. I was fascinated by the visibility of same-sex relationships among the members of a pop dance group. The dancers were all Indonesian domestic workers who made public displays of affection without inhibition, including holding hands, hugging, and kissing on the lips. They did not hide the fact that they were in a type of same-sex relationship common in Indonesian society, whereby a masculine-looking woman and a feminine-looking woman are clearly distinguishable. I wondered, what are the ideologies circulating in the migrant community that make same-sex relationships desirable, rather than a sign of mental illness, as in the case in Indonesia? How do these Indonesian women make sense of their sexuality in Hong Kong?

Previous studies on migrant communities tended to view them as a site of resistance (Constable 1997; Lan 2006; Yeoh and Huang 1998): migrant workers sit in public spaces and do as they please on their day off even though they are met with the disapproving stares of the locals. For example, migrant workers in Hong Kong would lay out a plastic mat along a pedestrian walkway and chat, eat meals, and do whatever they find relaxing. As noted by Constable (1997), these migrant women continue to enjoy their day off even if they attract dark looks from the local passers-by. This ability to ignore the locals in public spaces is interpreted by scholars as a form of resistance, although the migrant workers themselves seldom articulate their behavior in this manner but rather consider it a form of relaxation on their days off.

While the notion of resistance is useful for analyzing the tensions between the locals and the migrant workers as well as revealing the racial hierarchies in nonwork domains, the dynamics and organization within the migrant community have been overlooked, especially the meanings of their Sunday activities. I am interested in how their activities help migrant women make sense of their new gender image and sexuality; for instance, their Sunday dance competitions and fashion shows. I first examine the characteristics of the Indonesian migrant community in Hong Kong; for example, what the migrant community can offer Indonesian women, apart from serving as an outlet for socializing and relaxing. The discussion will focus on the pop dance groups formed by Indonesian migrant workers, particularly the gender knowledge produced by their activities.

The second part of the chapter will discuss the sexual ideologies that circulate in these pop dance groups. The discussion will shed light on the formation of the kin world that enables these Indonesian women to make sense of their new genders of *tomboi* and *cewek*. I will discuss the meanings of *tomboi* and how *tomboi* became a sexual identity among these women. The discussion will proceed to include how the women evaluate men, particularly Indonesian men, South Asian men, and Hong Kong men. Lastly, I will examine the lived experiences of Indonesian women who had no interest in women before. How do they change their thoughts about lesbianism from negative to desirable? How do they reconsider their sexuality when lesbianism presents itself as a desirable option? Given only one day off per week, how do they develop intimacy with their same-sex lover in Hong Kong?

Characteristics of Indonesian Migrant Community

Victoria Park and Kowloon Park

Both the Consulate General of the Republic of Indonesia and Bank Mandiri, the largest bank headquartered in Jakarta, are in Causeway Bay. Victoria Park, a five-minute walk from the Consulate General office, is one the largest parks in Hong Kong. The park is approximately the size of twenty soccer fields and spacious enough to accommodate thousands of Indonesians enjoying their day off, transforming Victoria Park and the streets nearby into Little Indonesia on Sundays. Shops that sell Indonesian food and salons that target Indonesians have flourished in that area. Aside from Victoria Park, Kowloon Park is another popular venue for Indonesians to gather on Sundays. The Kowloon Masjid and Islamic Centre is in the immediate vicinity of Kowloon Park. Paul O'Connor (2012) observed that Indonesian migrant workers spend their days off at the masjid.

Although Hong Kong people also make use of the two parks on Sundays, including the swimming pool, soccer pitches, basketball and tennis courts, and children's playgrounds, few Hong Kong people sit in the park for hours, besides the elderly. In addition to the various facilities, a lawn of about two hectares in size occupies the center of Victoria Park. On Sundays, Indonesian migrant women fill the park, find a space, lay out a plastic tablecloth for their food and drink, and enjoy their day off with their friends. Kowloon Park does not have a lawn but still provides ample space for Indonesian migrant women to enjoy refreshments with their friends.

Aside from these two parks, Indonesian migrant workers, like Hong Kong people, also shop, watch movies, and go to karaoke boxes for entertainment. However, the parameters of this study are mainly restricted to the parks because they are adequately large, a lot of Indonesian women frequent them, and most importantly, women spend relatively long hours there compared to shopping malls or fast-food eateries. The pop dance groups that I associated with during my fieldwork spent most of their days off at Victoria Park and Kowloon Park.

Encouraging voices of migrant women

Beyond serving the purposes of socializing and relaxation, the migrant domestic worker community and its activities also produce other meanings and has other impacts upon the migrant workers. One of the ways that they do this is to encourage migrant workers to find their voice. There are well-established Indonesian labor unions in Hong Kong, such as the Indonesian Migrant Workers Union and the Association of Indonesian Migrant Workers (ATKI). With support from regional migrant labor activists, such as the Asian Migrant Centre and Asian Migrants Coordinating Body, migrant workers of different ethnicities come together to work on labor issues (Wee and Sim 2005).

One of the implications of the growth of Indonesian migrant activism is that Indonesian women learn to openly voice their concerns about labor issues, such as the problems of underpayment and exorbitant agency fees. Indonesian labor unions have organized large-scale rallies and protest marches (typically hundreds of participants and sometimes up to a thousand). Waving flags, wearing eye-catching costumes, putting on dance performances, and singing revolutionary songs are primarily how these workers warm up as participants in these rallies and protests, as well as a way of attracting the attention of other Indonesian workers who have gathered at Victoria Park (Lai 2010).

Nevertheless, Constable noted that it took many years for Indonesian women to become emboldened enough to publicly march for their rights. A member of the ATKI told Constable the participants wore black masks when they launched their first-ever rally to protest their exploitation by employers, recruitment agencies, and the Indonesian government in 2001 out of fear of recognition and reprisal by the Indonesian government. In fact, the government did not take any follow-up action to punish anyone for organizing or participating in the protest, emboldening Indonesian migrant workers to face cameras and reporters during rallies and protests. None of the migrant worker participants covered themselves up in the anti–World Trade Organization demonstrations in 2005 (Constable 2010). During my fieldwork from 2010 to 2012, I did not see any Indonesian migrant worker cover her face in protests or processions. The increase in labor activism in the Indonesian migrant community has inspired more Indonesian women to find their voice.

Obtaining skills and knowledge

Indonesian migrant workers share a culture of membership-based groups in Hong Kong. There are many different types of groups for dance, religion, wealth management, labor rights, and so on. The parks that have more space allow groups to hold a wider range of activities, such as work meetings, sharing sessions, praying, and dancing. Group leaders and senior members who already have the skills and knowledge adopt the role of organizer and teach junior members. When junior members are experienced enough to teach other members, they then become the seniors. Some might leave the group and become the leader of a new group. The groups are solely run by the Indonesian women themselves.

It is worth noting that migrant women themselves are organized and bonded by membership in their particular group; they are not merely friends but adhere to the rules and regulations of the group. The groups are well structured with hierarchical positions, such as president, vice president, treasurer, secretary, and trainer. While the leader of the group holds the position of president, other positions are elected. Members vie for these positions. Membership is exclusive in that one should join only one group at a time. Appearing in another group would be considered a betrayal. Champion, the dance group I affiliated with, had a membership system in place. Member identity was clearly reflected by the monthly membership fee and uniform. Members are required to pay a monthly fee of HKD 20 (approx. USD 3) and buy a uniform. The group has both a summer uniform, which is a crew-neck tee, and a winter uniform, which is a hoodie. The front of the uniform is inscribed with the name "Champion" and the group's logo. The back is inscribed with the first name of the member. Members wear the uniform when they participate in a performance event, to show a sense of unity to the other dance groups.

To the Indonesian women in this study, these membership-based groups provide an ideal space to learn new skills and knowledge, opportunities not available to them in Indonesia. One of the Champion members recalled that in her childhood experience in Indonesia, only traditional singing and dancing were offered at school. Now she could learn pop dance. Apart from dance activities, Indonesian labor unions sometimes approach the dance groups to talk about labor rights and criticize the policies of the Indonesian government. The Indonesian women in this study recalled that their schools taught only about the positive contributions of the Indonesian government; no one in Indonesia would ever discuss politics or labor rights with them. The migrant community offers ample opportunities for these Indonesian women to learn new skills and knowledge in Hong Kong.

Pop Dance Group

One type of cultural group that is popular among Indonesian migrant women is the pop dance group. Their dance is a mix of dance-pop, hip-hop, and break dance. During my fieldwork, Lady Gaga and Korean boy bands, such as Super Junior and SHINee, were their favorites and objects of imitation. The dance groups caught my attention early on in my fieldwork because two genders, *tomboi* and *cewek*, are clearly distinguishable there. The *tomboi* dress in young men's clothing with short hair while the *cewek* dress in women's clothing, usually with longer, more feminine hairstyles. Moreover, same-sex relationships were common in dance groups. Couples openly expressed intimacy, such as hugging and kissing, and did not hide the fact that they were in a romantic relationship.

It would be a grave mistake to assume that only lesbians participate the pop dance groups. In fact, the dance groups welcome any Indonesian domestic worker who is interested in dancing. Therefore, participation in a dance group does not have any implications for sexual orientation. Women who do not have any same-sex relationships are welcome to join. The leader and members do not treat them any differently. For instance, Yaya, who is in her midtwenties, is not interested in women. Still, she is highly respected and was elected secretary of Champion.

I asked the migrant women in my study about the channels for joining Champion. Most said that friends who are already members referred them. Personal networking is the primary means of recruiting new members. While dancing is the major activity in the group, not every member is that keen about it. Some members joined the group to spend time with their member friends. In this sense, the pop dance groups also serve as outlets for the members to socialize. There is another way of joining the groups, which is to directly approach the group. Yanis (twenty-seven years old) said that when she first went to Victoria Park in 2004, she was fascinated by a group of Indonesian women who were dancing and singing together. Yanis wanted to join the group so she could dance with other Indonesian women, so she approached them and asked.

Pop dance groups spend a substantial amount of time and resources on performance events and competitions. Every well-established dance group aims to organize an annual event to mark its anniversary. This annual event is usually composed of (1) a *tomboi* fashion contest, (2) a *cewek* fashion contest, and (3) a pop dance competition. The ratio of the three groups of contestants (*tomboi*, *cewek*, and dance teams) is usually about 2:3:1. To earn a place to compete in the contests, each contestant or dance team is required to pay an HKD 100 (approx. USD 13) registration fee. The host group uses the money to pay for the venue and sound system rental, refreshments, gifts, and trophies. This kind of event is by no means small in scale and usually attracts approximately a hundred individuals and teams. The host group also uses its network to invite individuals outside of the community to act as judges for the contests. For example, a member attended a paid dance class taught by a Hong Kong instructor and later invited the instructor to act as the judge of the dance competition. The relationship is mutually beneficial—the host group flaunts the depth and breadth of its network, and the instructor takes the opportunity to recruit other Indonesian women for paid dance classes.

The Sunday activities and competitions confer *prestasi* (achievement) on the migrant women. According to Tom Boellstorff (2004b), *prestasi* is the manifestation of good citizenship in Indonesia. The distinguishing characteristics of *prestasi* are positive, and *prestasi* is meant to foster social connectivity. For example, *prestasi* can be a personal achievement that reflects favorably on one's community, such as succeeding in one's career. In return, the community acknowledges the achievement and recognizes the individual who did the good deed. The notion of *prestasi* is useful for explaining the prevalence of organizing and taking part in competitions in the Indonesian community. By participating in the competitions and winning a prize, members gain recognition in their own group. Well-established groups gain recognition in the migrant community by organizing a large-scale competition and inviting more than a hundred people to take part in the competition. Indonesian women highly value their *prestasi*, even in Hong Kong. Membership in a pop dance group is an active process driven by the notion of *prestasi*, in which the migrant women aim to do good deeds and aspire to acknowledgment from their group members and the community.

Creativity is another element highly valued in the competitions. Contestants are required to create their own fashion style or dance steps. I observed that the word *kreatifitas* (creativity) was used as part of either the theme or slogan on the backdrop of the stage, for example:

- Color your life full of creativity (Warnai hidupmu penuh kreasi)
- Show your perfect creativity (Tunjukkan kreasimu untuk menjadi jati diri yang sempurna)
- Enhancing our creativity (Untuk menggalang kreativitas anak-anak negeri)

The fashion show and dance contests highly encourage Indonesian migrant women to imagine themselves differently—beyond the subject position of migrant domestic worker and her present, routine daily life.

Tomboi and *Cewek* in Performance

The fashion show and dance competition are crucial arenas for producing a new gender ideology, in which *tomboi* is recognized as a gender category apart from "women." The host group offers separate divisions for *tomboi* and *cewek*. The two divisions, "*tomboi* fashion" and "*cewek* fashion," have equal importance and are considered each other's counterparts. The promotional flyer will clearly list the two divisions; therefore, the *tomboi* contestants understand that they should register for *"tomboi* fashion."

The first competition that I attended was called *"Tomboi* Funky" (*Tomboi* fashion) and "Miss Evening Dress" (*Cewek* fashion). The *tomboi* contestants expressed the "funky" theme by wearing young men's clothing and gothic-style makeup, leather boots, and heavy metal accessories. All of them walked with large strides and did not smile. The *cewek* contestants, in contrast, wore evening dresses and smiled brightly, making feminine gestures, such as putting one hand on their waist as they walked. I also attended a fashion show with a summer theme. The *cewek* who was awarded champion in the fashion show wore a low-cut dress with a floral pattern and a garland on her head with vibrant pink, yellow, white, and purple flowers. The *tomboi* who was awarded champion wore a designer men's shirt and a pair of shorts, both in vivid colors. This *tomboi*, like many other of the *tomboi* contestants, wore aviator sunglasses when performing on stage.

When I expressed my interest in the differentiation between *tomboi* and *cewek* in the fashion contest, the vice president of Champion, who is a *tomboi*, responded:

> This is normal [*Biasa saja*]. There are *tomboi* and *cewek*. So, there are fashion contests for both *tomboi* and *cewek*.

The gender difference is clearly depicted and produced by dividing the competition into *tomboi* and *cewek*. The comment made by the vice president suggests that it is a norm for pop dance groups to hold separate divisions for *tomboi* and *cewek* because the ways they dress and walk are different. By differentiating the two genders (*tomboi* and *cewek*) and organizing separate divisions for them, the gender difference is clearly maintained and observed by the pop dance groups.

When the members of these pop dance groups deliberate on who should compete in the two divisions, the dialogue also shapes gender identification. During my fieldwork, I decided to take part in a fashion contest organized by Champion. Several weeks before the event, Michelle, the leader of Champion, was working on the event schedule to register the participants in their divisions. Michelle thought that I was a *tomboi* because of my short hair and men's clothing and asked me whether I was going to compete in the *tomboi* division. I intentionally responded that I had not decided yet. I wanted to know how she would react to my indecisive attitude, which suggested the possibility of my participation in the *cewek* division. Michelle assured me that it was my decision. However, my indecisiveness turned into a topic of discussion among the group members. On the following Sunday, I met with the Champion group members at Victoria Park as usual. April (twenty-six, *cewek*) asked me, "Do you want to be a *cewek*?" She laughed and continued, "You'll need a wig then." Alexis (twenty-eight, *cewek*) followed suit and said, "You're tall and thin. Don't compete in the *cewek* division. You would look better as a *tomboi* in the *tomboi* division."

Michelle seemed to respect my indecisiveness but could not stop herself from sharing my possible participation in the *cewek* division with others behind my back. April teased me, and Alexis advised me that my "tall and thin" appearance would better fit the masculine ideal in the *tomboi* fashion contest. In doing so, their aim was to inform me that my participation in the *cewek* division would be strange and unacceptable. By gossip, teasing, and persuasion, they tried to entice my compliance with the rules of the game, that is, a *tomboi* should take part in the *tomboi* division. Although Michelle had assured me that I could *choose* between the two divisions, this was a bluff indeed. I was pressured to identify with one gender category. Her sharing with others ultimately marked *tomboi* as a gender, or the counterpart of *cewek*. The repetitive act of organizing separate divisions for *tomboi* and *cewek* confirms and reinforces the boundary between the two genders in the community.

Gender appearance and image on stage are also transferred from the senior members to the newer ones. The senior members of Champion were responsible for teaching and helping the newer members embrace the attributes of a certain gender. Alexis (twenty-eight, *cewek*) interpreted my indecisive attitude toward participating in the *tomboi* or *cewek* division as my lack of skill in walking the catwalk as a *tomboi*:

> "If you don't know how to walk the catwalk as a *tomboi*, I can show you." Alexis then stood up and demonstrated the *tomboi* catwalk with verbal instructions: "Clench your fists when you're walking, see? Be cool, no smiling." She then pointed to her chest and said, "Keep this flat."

Although Alexis is a *cewek*, she knows the skills and aesthetics needed for a *tomboi* to win in a fashion show after attending these performance events for years. As a senior member of Champion, she took on the responsibility of teaching me how to walk the catwalk as a *tomboi*. She informed me that masculine attributes, including a flat chest, unsmiling expression, and clenched fists, are the basics for a *tomboi* on the catwalk.

I eventually decided to participate in the *tomboi* division. I told Alexis that I had no suitable clothes for fashion contest and needed her advice on shopping for the theme of *tomboi* funky. Alexis promised to help with no hesitation. We went to Kwai Chung Plaza[1] with another *tomboi* to shop for clothes and accessories for the fashion contest. Alexis was patient and provided suggestions when we shopped, and she selected all the clothes and the necklace I wore for the fashion contest. One of the Champion members styled my hair and painted my lips and cheeks in gray to fit the funky theme.

---

1. Kwai Chung Plaza is famous for its small shops and low prices. It sells fashionable clothes and trendy products with compromised quality.

My experience is not unique. I observed a *tomboi* practicing the catwalk on her own in a quiet corner of the park. The *tomboi* tried to look distant and cold and clenched her fists when she was walking, but she was not very good at it and instead burst into laughter in the middle of her walk. The vice president of Champion had also been standing and watching the *tomboi* for a while. I guessed that she wanted to help the *tomboi* improve her performance. However, both burst into laughter when the vice president mocked the way that the *tomboi* was walking.

In addition to teaching how to walk the catwalk, senior members also do makeup and hair for newer members. The makeup for *tomboi* consists of drawing facial hair, thick eyebrows, and temporary tattoos. I observed that the newer members never objected to or complained about their makeup. Within the group, the junior members learn the gender attributes of *tomboi* and *cewek* from the seniors.

The two genders, *tomboi* and *cewek*, are institutionalized by organizing separate divisions for them. The members of pop dance groups maintain the boundary of the two genders by scrutinizing each other's choice of division for competition. Anyone who does not follow the rules of the game, that *tomboi* should compete in the *tomboi* division and *cewek* in the *cewek* division, deserves to be teased and become the object of gossip. The boundary that divides *cewek* and *tomboi* is reinforced when the seniors demonstrate the catwalk and do the makeup and hair of the newer members. The pop dance groups therefore produce and disseminate gender knowledge to their members by participating in performance events.

Pop dance groups do not isolate themselves from the larger Indonesian migrant community. They participate in activities organized by other Indonesian groups if they are a good fit. Indonesian labor unions also organize performance events and short play contests on the theme of labor rights at Victoria Park. The contestants don costumes or use slogans that symbolize the plight as well as the rights of migrant domestic workers. According to these migrant labor unions, organizing performance events with the theme of labor rights is one of their strategies to reach out to the migrant workers and disseminate information on their rights in Hong Kong. Pop dance groups also participate in this kind of performance event, as they really enjoy performing on stage.

In terms of the short play contests, the contestants are required to create a scripted play that incorporates dancing and songs on the theme of labor rights. The plot of the play is usually about the greed of the Indonesian government in sending women nationals to work abroad without adequate legal protection, the suffering of Indonesian migrant workers in Hong Kong, and how they address these problems by uniting. A play usually involves around fifteen people, who play different roles, from cold-hearted Indonesian government officials, the recruitment agency, abusive employers, migrant labor unions, to the Indonesian workers.

Although their original purpose was to disseminate information on migrant labor rights, the short plays unexpectedly increased the visibility of *tomboi* who performed the male roles on stage. When Champion competed in a short play contest, I was cast in a male role and paired with a *cewek* to act as a Hong Kong couple who made unreasonable demands on their Indonesian migrant domestic worker. On the day of the competition, I wore a shirt and tie to indicate my status as an employer. However, it was not enough. I was reminded by a *cewek* member to tuck the bottom of my shirt into my pants so that my dress code would pass as that of a white-collar, middle-class male employer. There was also another *tomboi* member who performed as a male employer. Yet another *tomboi* acted as a male staff member of a recruitment agent company. The two *tomboi* and I never exchanged ideas on what we were going to wear. Yet interestingly, we all wore the same style of clothing on the day of the contest: a shirt and tie, pants with a belt, and a pair of glasses. In addition to Champion, the other pop dance groups also assigned their *tomboi* members to play the men's roles on stage.

Tomboi masculinity is considered not threatening but a routine part of the performance events that are prevalent in the migrant community. Since the performance events held at Victoria Park are highly accessible to the larger migrant community, *tomboi* performing as men on stage and wearing men's clothing have become commonplace in the migrant community.

The Kin World

The pop dance groups perceive themselves as a family unit composed of a mother, father, sisters, and brothers. The leaders and members use kin terms to address each other, depending on whether the person is a *tomboi* or *cewek*, and on seniority—the age of the person and years spent in the group. For instance, Michelle (thirty-two years old, *cewek*), as the leader of Champion, takes on the role of the mother. Her *tomboi* partner, Eddy (twenty-nine years old), has the role of the father. The leader and her opposite-gender partner are the parents of the dance group. The other members see each other as siblings. The older *tomboi* are the older brothers, and older *cewek* are the older sisters. The kin relationship among the members of the dance group is highly gendered. It is worth noting that the practice of using kin terms and defining the group as a family is not constructed by the pop dance groups themselves. Rather, the practice is an Indonesian tradition, family-ism (kekeluargaan), established in the 1920s by the Indonesian nationalists to counter Dutch colonialism in the 1920s. While the Indonesian nationalists saw the Dutch establishment of bureaucracy and organizations with official regulations as a desirable form of modernization, they emphasized that organizations should not lose family values, which unite people by the heart and not merely by regulations (Shiraishi 1997). Therefore, kin relationships are commonly used in government and corporate organizations to describe and position relationships between seniors and juniors. This historical context provides a window for understanding the popularity of using kin terms among the Indonesian groups.

The practice of using kin terms to address each other subject every member to either a *tomboi* or *cewek* position. The gender knowledge of *tomboi* and *cewek* is not limited to only onstage performance but embodied in their daily interactions. Champion made plans to hold a picnic at a beach on a Sunday afternoon. The day before, a member sent out a group text message, which listed the names of the *tomboi* members, including the father of Champion's and my names. The message asked all the *tomboi* to wear a pink bikini on the day of the picnic. This humorous text message identified the *tomboi* by name. It also regulated the gender behavior of *tomboi* by assuming that *tomboi* would be reluctant to wear a bikini because it would contradict their masculine identity. The text message discursively produced those who are *tomboi* and a taboo that *tomboi* should avoid.

On the day of the picnic, the two genders, *tomboi* and *cewek*, were further enacted when a member proposed taking a group picture of the *cewek*. The fifteen *cewek* immediately came together and posed: some mimicked a flower and had both hands opened under their face; many put one hand on their waist. All of them smiled. The *tomboi* seemed to be inspired. A *tomboi* said that she also wanted a group picture. So, the *tomboi* immediately came together. Instead of putting their hand on their waist, the *tomboi* put one hand on their thigh to show their muscles and strength. All of them put on a stern expression. Their gendered postures for the photos were consistent with those for the fashion contests.

By incorporating the members into a family structure, every Champion member is socialized according to shared gender knowledge of *tomboi* and *cewek*. The ultimate effect of establishing the kin world is that every member is marked by her perceived gender. The text message that teased the *tomboi* about wearing a bikini and the separate group pictures of the *tomboi* and *cewek* demonstrated that every member should know her own gender position and act accordingly.

Kin labor

Champion, as a family unit, did not own any physical space, such as a room in a dormitory or an apartment. Their kin relations were maintained and embodied by kin labor instead of the physical space of a home. In his study on butch queens and the ballroom culture in Detroit, Marlon Bailey noted that kinship is common among the ballroom houses. Close friends in the black LGBT community formed a ballroom house and participated in performance events organized by other ballroom houses. Bailey (2013) argued that ballroom houses emphasized the activity of creating kin without relying on a fixed space. The activity of creating kin, or kin labor, includes the provision of social support, protection from homophobic violence, and parenting. While I am aware that there is no direct cultural connection between the ballroom houses in Detroit and the pop dance groups, I am inspired by Bailey's notion of the "labor of parenting" because it is useful for understanding how the kin ties of pop dance groups are maintained even though neither blood ties nor the physical space of a home exists.

Parents are expected to fulfill their roles and provide the actual labor of parenting, such as giving advice whenever any member has labor issues, conflict with other members, or relationship problems. Parenting has two major forms: members can directly approach the parent when they need advice, or the parent takes the initiative to talk to members when she becomes aware of an issue. Labor issues are common among Indonesian migrant domestic workers. Since they do not have any coworkers in the home of their employer, they usually wait until Sunday to seek advice from their parents. A twenty-three-year-old member approached Michelle, the mother of Champion, to share that her employer did not regularly provide her with food. Despite this unreasonable treatment, she did not want to resign because her contract was almost finished. A standard contract between a migrant domestic worker and her employer is two years. Within the two years, both parties have the right to terminate the contract. The side that terminates the contract is responsible for paying one month of salary to the other side as compensation. This member did not want to compensate her employer, so she wanted to finish out the contract despite the unreasonable treatment. After listening to the story, Michelle neither encouraged her to resign nor dismissed her complaint. Instead, Michelle urged her to think twice. Then, Michelle handed a blank form to this member and told her that if she decided to quit she needed to complete the form and submit it to her employer as a letter of resignation; otherwise, the employer could sue her for leaving without giving formal notice.

Michelle also reached out whenever her members encountered problems. For instance, April (twenty-six, *cewek*) lost her job and was forced to live on a tight budget while staying at a venue arranged by her recruitment agency. April avoided socializing with Champion members because she did not have the money for transportation or eating out. April told me that Michelle called her on a Sunday morning:

> You know, I don't want the people in Champion to know that I don't have money. It's very embarrassing. But Michelle is very nice. She called me this morning and said that she can meet me at my place and then we can go to Victoria Park together. She said that she would pay for me. But I didn't want to [accept her offer] because I'm embarrassed. I told Michelle that I would not go. But Michelle knew what I was thinking. She persuaded me not to feel embarrassed about her offer. She said that we are family and shouldn't feel bad. So, that's why I came today.

As the mother of Champion, Michelle provides both guidance and care to her children. By guidance, I am referring to the advice that she gives to her children, such as reminding a mistreated member about the proper procedure for resignation in Hong Kong. By care, I am referring to both the emotional and financial support that Michelle offered April. April emphasized that Michelle was very caring and assuaged her feelings of embarrassment. In her labor of parenting, Michelle did not confine herself to the conventional role of mother, as endorsed by the Indonesian government since the 1970s. The middle-class feminine ideal in Indonesia is to become a housewife (Silvey 2004). Mothers are not expected to give career advice to their children, although they are responsible for conveying moral beliefs to their children. Michelle, as the mother of Champion, was doing both. Michelle provided both career advice and emotional support to her two children. By carrying out the labor of parenting, Michelle maintained the kin relations and encouraged her children to trust and rely on her.

Changing Meanings of *Tomboi*: Sex and Desires

Tomboi is not a new word to most Indonesians. It is a common term in Indonesia, referring to a young, unmarried girl with boyish behaviors, someone who, for instance, refuses to wear dresses and is physically active in sports. Being called a *tomboi* may not necessarily imply a young woman's sexuality, such as desiring another woman, but is used as an adjective to describe her gender appearance and behavior that do not meet the feminine ideal. Nevertheless, the term *tomboi* does imply the same-sex sexuality of a woman in specific communities. For example, Evelyn Blackwood (2010) noted that women in a community in West Sumatra, Indonesia, who desire women used the term *tomboi* to refer to themselves. The Indonesian women in this study also used *tomboi* to refer to masculine women who are attracted to women. Therefore, *tomboi* is not merely a term to indicate the gender appearance of a young woman but also a marker of same-sex sexuality in the context of this study.

I do not take the status quo definition of *tomboi* because I am interested in examining the relationship between the migratory processes and the changing meanings of *tomboi*. Therefore, I will focus on the stories of the migrant women at the training centers in Indonesia in the following section. The stories will shed light on how Indonesian women learn and produce new meanings of *tomboi*, which further shape their interactions and same-sex desires in the migrant community in Hong Kong.

Policing of sex in the training centers

Before leaving for Hong Kong, Indonesian migrant women are required to stay at a single-sex training center for months to learn to speak Cantonese and gain job-related skills, such as cooking Chinese food. The women are not allowed to leave the training center until the day they depart for Hong Kong. This is to secure the transition; that is, to ensure that they will not become pregnant or leave to use another recruitment agency (Lindquist 2009a). Recruitment agencies are concerned about the problem of pregnancy because any migrant worker who is found pregnant in the host country is sent back to Indonesia immediately, costing the agency money. Therefore, it is common practice for recruitment agencies to confine the women to the training center. There might be just one or two men working in the management office; all trainers are women.

The construction of a single-sex environment prevents heterosexual but not same-sex intimacy. At *pesantren* (Islamic boarding schools) in Indonesia, female students are restricted to a single-sex environment to preserve their sexual morality. But as revealed by previous studies, same-sex relationships between female students exist inside *pesantren* (Kholifah 2006; Mustaghfiroh 2014; Nurish 2010). Amanah Nurish (2010) conducted participant observations in a *pesantren* and found a *kakak-adik* (older sister–younger sister) form of erotic relationships between female students, in which a *kakak* preferred male clothing and projected a responsible image protecting her *adik*. Nurish sometimes saw a *kakak* and *adik* kissing in an empty room. Students were cautious to hide their same-sex relationships from the *pesantren* leaders because they knew that they would be expelled if they were caught.

Amy Sim discussed the occurrence of same-sex relationships between Indonesian migrant women in the training centers. Sim theorized that same-sex relationships in training centers were caused by loneliness and harsh living conditions. She wrote that "these conditions resonate with studies of homosexuality in total institutions like prisons, and boarding schools and so forth" (Sim 2010, 46). Her argument that a coerced single-sex environment plus harsh living conditions cause same-sex relationships seems to follow the sexual deprivation model in prison studies, which suggests that inmates are deprived of "normal" heterosexual sex; therefore, they seek same-sex intimacy with other inmates. Although the sexual deprivation model was well received in prison studies during the period from the 1940s to the 1960s, Barth (2012) pointed out that the proponents of the deprivation model have never provided any empirical proof through scientific study. Instead of asking a *why* question concerning the causes of homosexuality in training centers, I am more interested in exploring what gender knowledge is produced in the training centers and how it enables same-sex relationships.

Michel Foucault reminds us that the modern form of policing of sex incites individuals to speak about sex, especially forbidden sex, in the form of confession to authority figures, including teachers, priests, doctors, and parents. Sexuality is managed through procedures—constant observation, interrogation, confession, and punishment. Foucault also notes that the ways that sex is regulated do not stop individuals from engaging in forbidden sex; rather, they produce detailed descriptions of individuals who practice forbidden sex. If a case of sodomy is uncovered by a priest, those involved are interrogated, forced to give details about their childhood and their life, in addition to describing their sexual acts and desires. The detailed descriptions are used to form the category of homosexuality, its reality and intelligibility. Homosexuality is "a species with specification," not merely the practice of same-sex acts (Foucault 1984, 323). The notion of sex policing will be useful for understanding how the trainers sexualize the space of the training centers by banning same-sex behaviors. The following will examine how a "desexual" marker (i.e., a ban on same-sex relationships) becomes a catalyst for producing the discourse of "*tomboi* desiring women."

According to the Indonesian women in this study, there are *tomboi* in the training centers. They noted that the trainers take an active role in identifying those who are *tomboi* and give them special treatment based on the assumption that *tomboi* are sexually attracted to women and disturb other women at night. For example, the trainers either assign the identified *tomboi* to sleep on the upper bunk of the bunk beds or separate them in another bedroom at night. The practice marks *tomboi* as a category; those who belong to this category are subjected to extra surveillance. The trainers are authorized to punish anyone who is found having sexual contact with another woman. The way that these trainers handle situations with women who are involved in a same-sex relationship approximates Foucault's notion of the "policing of sex"—constant observation, interrogation, confession, and punishment.

I asked the women in my study how the trainers could differentiate a *tomboi* when all the women looked almost the same in their uniform and given the same short haircut once admitted to the training center. They told me that the trainers differentiated *tomboi* from their unfeminine attitude and behavior. One of the behaviors that was said to be a trait of a *tomboi* was taking care of one woman over a long period of time, such as queuing in line to get food for her and spending time with her during lunch breaks and after work. The women in my study also said that *tomboi* flirt, gaze at, and even touch their object of interest. A point worth noting is that these characteristics of *tomboi* are not solely produced by the trainers but also produced in the daily conversations of the women themselves. The ban provoked the women to talk about sex between women.

Lestari (thirty-five years old, married) said that there were many *tomboi* at her training center who were kept under open surveillance. Lestari was mistaken as a *tomboi* by her trainers. She described how her trainers monitored her:

> The trainers were always looking at me. It made me feel that they didn't like me. At night, they made me sleep on the top bunk. The people on the bottom bunk were able to watch me.

The following incident showed how the surveillance of *tomboi* incited Lestari and other Indonesian women in the training center to talk about *tomboi* sexuality. Lestari said:

> My training center was haunted. One night, there was a strange noise which sounded like someone was riding a horse. Everyone was frightened. A woman came over to my bed. When the trainers came by, I told them, "it's not my fault. She came to me herself."

In this incident, the trainers quickly interrogated Lestari when they saw a woman in her bed. The trainers assumed that Lestari was a *tomboi* and so she was the seducer. Therefore, the trainers interrogated Lestari but not the woman who went over to her bed. In the interrogation, a *tomboi* sharing a bed with another woman was constructed as form of homosexual behavior. Speech about homosexual behavior was incited. Other women overheard the interrogation, as it took place publicly in the common bedroom. This could further incite those who overheard the interrogation to gossip about Lestari's sexuality and the characteristics of *tomboi*.

Talking, including interrogation and gossip, produces truth (Foucault 1984). The policing of sex—constant observation and interrogation—produces the characteristics of *tomboi*: *tomboi* desire and seduce women in the absence of their trainers. In turn, the specification of *tomboi* is seen as the truth and knowledge of gender that reinforces the legitimacy of the practice—*tomboi* deserve extra surveillance. Whether the trainers can correctly identify a *tomboi* is not relevant; rather, what the trainers and the women say about the sexuality of the *tomboi* is the key to understanding the construction process of *tomboi* at the training centers.

Investing in the *tomboi* subject position

In this section, I examine how the women identify with the *tomboi* subject position. How do they come to see themselves as *tomboi*? Based on their personal stories, I examine how the discourse of *tomboi* desiring women circulating in the training centers prompts women to reassess their gender identity and sexual desire. On the one hand, how do they come to identify themselves as a *tomboi* in the training center? While I look at the influence of the new experiences on the transformation of their sexual subjectivity, I also examine their past experiences, particularly their relationship with their boyfriend or husband, in shaping their current practices. On the other hand, how do they use the new discourse to modify the meanings of their former relationships with men?

I borrow Nathaniel Lewis's notion of migration as a life change to prompt personal reassessment (2012, 221). In his study of gay men in the United States, Lewis argued that coming out is not a single moment but a more gradual and accretive process. The gay men in his study experienced segmented journeys, such as taking several return trips between the childhood home and a potential "queer home," before coming out as gay men. Migration provided opportunities for these gay men to distance themselves from heterosexual relationships and realize the possibility of a different life. These opportunities prompted personal reassessment and contributed to a new sexual subjectivity in a gradual, accretive process. Although I do not examine the coming out process of the Indonesian women in this study, Lewis's work offers insight into the impact of new gender and sexual ideologies during the migratory processes on reshaping the sexuality of these women.

One's subject position may shift in the process of reassessment. Individuals are subjected to conflicting discourses, including past experiences and current circumstances. The notion of habitus as used by Pierre Bourdieu is useful here for understanding the formation of sexual subjectivity from a temporal perspective—past experiences are alive and shape new experiences; new experiences can modify past experiences. Bourdieu (1990) emphasized the weight of past experiences in current practices because past experiences constitute the unconscious part of ourselves. The notion of habitus will be used to examine the past experiences of these Indonesian women, particularly their relationship with their boyfriend or husband, in shaping their current practices and experiences: How do they use the new discourse to modify the meanings of their former relationships with men?

To better understand the processes of individual adoption of *tomboi* identity, I used the theory of the subject by Henrietta Moore. Moore (1994) used the concept of "investment" to explain why some individuals perform a gender that does not conform to the culturally defined model. This investment is an emotional commitment to a certain subject position that provides the individual with pleasure or emotional satisfaction. However, this investment in an alternative gender identity might come at the expense of social power, social approval, and even material benefits. Moore explained that subjectivity is multiple and contradictory; therefore, the theory of rational choice cannot explain why an individual would take up multiple subject positions that might be contradictory. Moore noted that adopting an identity is about not just the construction of self-identity but also interrelations with other individuals (namely, intersubjectivity); that is, the position assigned by other individuals. When the pleasure and emotional satisfaction gained from this particular position are very strong and appealing, the individual invests in it despite social disapproval. In this sense, interrelations with other individuals determine the position that one adopts.

The *tomboi* in this study told me that they were called *tomboi* in their home village because they refuse to present themselves in a feminine style, such as growing their hair to shoulder length and wearing dresses. They had short hair, about eight inches in length, when I meet them in Hong Kong. Fifteen of the twenty-four *tomboi* in this study said that since childhood, they had not been interested in feminine attire or long hair. Seven became aware of their interest in women around the age of twelve, but none had ever started a relationship with a woman, nor did they articulate the desire to develop a same-sex relationship before they went to the training centers. Actually, these seven women had been confused by their feelings toward women, so they did not disclose the information to anyone. Although they had been called *tomboi* in their home village, they did not consider it their sexual identity yet because they did not know anyone, neither girlfriends nor other *tomboi*, who recognized that *tomboi* desire women. The term *tomboi* to them was only an adjective that described their differences from other women, including gender appearance and their feelings toward women; it was not yet a subject position that they invested in until they encountered new romantic or sexual experiences at the training centers that prompted them to reassess their sexuality.

Joe (twenty-two years old, unmarried)

The story of Joe will show how she reassessed her sexuality after she was approached by a woman at a training center. Joe recognized her attraction to women when she was eleven. She said that she had feelings for pretty girls, "although I didn't understand it was a feeling of love [*cinta*] . . . the feeling is just different." Despite realizing her sexuality at an early age, Joe never revealed her feelings to other girls. She lacked a role model in the media or among her friends, so was unable to make sense of her attraction to women. Therefore, she decided not to disclose her feelings to anyone. During high school, she was approached by boys. Like many of her female classmates, Joe saw dating between boys and girls as normal and desirable. Therefore, she dated the boys who pursued her.

A trainer at her training center often took care of her. After leaving the training center, Joe received a profession of love in the form of a text message from this trainer. Joe was also attracted to her. So, they started a long-distance relationship and relied on text messages and phone calls to communicate. However, this relationship did not last long. The trainer soon developed a crush on another *tomboi* at her training center. After the relationship ended, Joe began to pursue women while she worked in Hong Kong. She positioned herself as a *tomboi* and as the boyfriend in all of her relationships with women.

In the past, Joe had not known that it was possible to have a romantic relationship with a woman because every romantic relationship in her experience was between a man and a woman. The profession of love via text message prompted Joe to reassess her sexuality. Joe recognized that love between women is possible because a woman had professed her love to Joe.

In the process of this reassessment, Joe compared her feelings toward women to her feelings toward men. She recalled her past dating experiences with men:

> When I was with men, I didn't feel my heart beating. I didn't like them very much. It's more like just going out with them. When I am with women, I'm much happier. For example, when I was with a boy, I wanted 90 percent, but the boy would only give me 60 percent. I didn't feel comfortable. But when

> I am with a girl, I give 100 percent and the girl would also give me more of herself. Actually, I was really into one of my boyfriends. I liked him very much because he played rock and roll. But our relationship lasted for only three months. We broke up because he wanted me to be girlish with longer hair and wear dresses. But I just couldn't. So, we broke up.

Joe did not want to perform femininity, so she refused to fulfill her boyfriend's request. In contrast, she enjoyed her role as a boyfriend while in a relationship with a woman:

> I like to spoil [*manja*] [someone in a relationship] rather than being spoiled [*dimanja*] [by someone in a relationship]. I am romantic. I show that I care for my girl. I enjoy creating surprises for my girl.

The above narratives show how Joe began to reconsider her sexuality after she was approached by a woman at the training center. It enabled Joe to rethink her childhood crushes on girls. Moreover, it also allowed Joe to realize that she could play an alternative role in a relationship—not as a girlfriend but as a boyfriend. Interestingly, her past relationships with men were not forgotten but remained alive to shape her new experiences with women. By comparing old experiences with new ones, which Joe found more pleasurable, she affirmed her same-sex attraction and *tomboi* subject position.

Iman (thirty-two years old, married, mother of a daughter)

Iman had her first sexual experience with a woman at the training center. This experience prompted her to reassess her sexuality. Early in 1998, Iman married her husband, and she has a daughter. Her family was very well off, but her husband lost his job in 1999 when Indonesia's economy of suffered severely from the Asian financial crisis. In 2003, Iman decided to become a migrant domestic worker to earn the money to finance bribes for her husband to get a job in Indonesia. That was her original motivation for working overseas.

Before her first sexual encounter with a woman at the training center, Iman had no knowledge about sex between two women:

> I was stupid. I didn't understand those things. At night, I saw the beds shaking after the lights were out, but I had no idea what it was all about.

Iman did not know there could be sex between two women until a woman made love to her.

> A trainer always looked at me when I went to bed. I wanted to avoid her, so I moved to another bed. There was another woman who reassured me that it was all right to sleep in that bed. I didn't know that she was a lesbian. In the middle of the night, she came over to make love to me! I didn't know what was going on but just felt my heart beating. Her breasts were very big. I was aroused by her. I never had that feeling before. My heart was beating so

strongly. . . . That was my first time, so I didn't really know what was going on. My heart was just beating so strongly. She wanted to take off my clothes. I kissed her back.

Iman was soon transferred to another building after she was selected by a Hong Kong employer. Iman did not see this woman again until both of them arrived in Hong Kong. Iman continued to meet and have sex with this woman despite having a husband and a daughter in Indonesia.

Her recollection of her heart beating strongly during her first sexual encounter with a woman prompted Iman to reconsider her sexuality. In the past, Iman never questioned her sexuality because she followed an ordinary life cycle: marrying a man and having children. Sex between two women was unfathomable to Iman; she could not make sense of the bed-shaking at the training center. After her first sexual encounter at the training center, Iman was surprised by her strong feelings, which she never experienced with her husband. This prompted Iman to reconsider her relationship with him:

> I don't think I really love my husband. I never felt my heart beating for him. My first love is the woman at the training center who made my heart beat so strongly.

Iman began to invest in the *tomboi* subject position when her lover expected her to be on top and take an active role in sex. Iman did not know what to do except to kiss her back. The woman then taught Iman sexual skills. Iman said:

> I was not so bright. She knew that it was my first time, so she taught me slowly. Then, I became smarter.

Iman's narrative highlights the active role of *tomboi* in bed as a cultural construction rather than a "natural" masculine desire. She fulfilled the expectation by learning new sexual skills. Her story demonstrates how an unexpected but pleasurable sexual experience can lead a woman to radically transform her sexuality—from a married woman to a *tomboi*.

Andra (twenty-six years old, married, no children)

At the age of twenty, Andra was forced by her family to marry a man whom she had never met. Three weeks after the marriage, her husband went to Jakarta to work. Andra did not want to live with her husband's family while he was gone. At the time, she was aware that working overseas might provide an opportunity for her to leave. Therefore, she asked permission from her husband to work overseas. Andra stayed at the training center for a whole year until a Hong Kong employer selected her for employment. During that year, Andra started relationships with women; also, she was told that her husband had a new wife and children in Jakarta. The opportunity to leave became the catalyst to invest in the *tomboi* subject position. Before discussing how this became the catalyst, I will address how Andra viewed her sexuality prior to entering the training center.

The idea of a *tomboi* who desires women was not a new concept to Andra, who grew up in a large city. There were two *tomboi* in her junior high school. In addition to having masculine short hair, Andra observed that these two *tomboi* spent most of their time with boys and had romantic relationships with girls in school. Andra herself had a crush on one of her classmates:

> Although I am a girl and had long hair, I am attracted to girls. I am a *tomboi*, not a real [*asli*] girl. But she [her crush] liked another girl. After we graduated, we didn't contact each other anymore.

Andra did not consider herself to be "a real girl" because she had feelings for one of her female classmates but never for boys. As Andra observed in school, *tomboi* are not "real girls" because they do things that girls do not do, including having short hair, spending time with boys, and desiring girls. She also noted that the girls who were attracted to the two *tomboi* looked feminine. This high school observation stayed with her and became part of her self-identification. Andra considered herself a *tomboi* because she was doing something that was similar to what the two *tomboi* in her school did—desiring feminine women.

The opportunity to leave her husband and his family prompted Andra to reconsider her sexuality. At the training center, Andra had two same-sex relationships. According to Andra, her girlfriends were feminine women. Pairing with feminine women affirmed her *tomboi* identity:

> Because I am a *tomboi*, those who like me are *cewek*. They are beautiful. . . . [Before coming to the training center,] I already had the feeling. It's the feeling where I feel half *tomboi* / half girl [*setengah tomboi setengah cewek*]. After separating from my man, I felt like a *tomboi*.

In the process of reassessing her sexuality, she had two subject positions: the first one is *tomboi* and the second is wife. In the past, she considered herself to be "half *tomboi*" because of her desire for feminine women. However, she did not see herself as a "complete" *tomboi* because she had not yet acted on her desire. As noted by Moore, "One's interrelationships with other individuals—intersubjectivity—will determine what positions one takes up" (1994, 65). Andra needed her object of desire to confirm her *tomboi* position, which did not happen until she went to the training center. In addition, her intersubjectivity as a wife was reduced at the training center. She did not want to invest in the wife subject position anymore because her husband cheated on her. She wanted liberation from this position, which had never really been one of her choice. The chance to leave her husband enabled Andra to completely invest in the *tomboi* subject position while at the same time discarding her wife identity.

Gender and Sexuality in the Migrant Community 59

Eddy (twenty-nine years old, unmarried)

Eddy had not had any boyfriends or husbands before being admitted to the training center, but her story is still significant for how past experiences in Indonesia shaped her understanding of same-sex attraction in the training center. Eddy came from a rural area. She told me that women in her village usually wear a *jilbab*, so she followed their example and wore a *jilbab* and shoulder-length hair. She also went to the mosque every day. Despite her compliance with this gender image, Eddy had been aware of her interest in women since childhood but never told anyone about it. After being admitted into the training center, for the first time she saw women in same-sex relationships. Eddy found herself attracted to a woman, who in turn was also attracted to Eddy. However, Eddy did not fully enact her *tomboi* subject position by being sexually forward. Instead, she refrained from it while still at the training center:

> At the training center, she liked me, and I also liked her. But it was not like having a relationship in Hong Kong. I was still shy. Shy about holding hands. Shy about kissing. People were doing these things at the training center. But there is still *adat* [an Indonesian concept referring to traditional culture, including customary practices and ideals]. *Adat* does not allow woman-with-woman. Woman-with-woman only happens in the training center. There is nothing like this in Indonesia.

Her narrative reveals two reassessment processes. First, the new gender discourse and woman-woman dating practices that Eddy witnessed at the training center prompted her to reassess her sexuality. In the past, Eddy had concealed any romantic feelings for women. At the training center, she decided to reveal her feelings for a woman she was attracted to. Second, Eddy was constrained from completely investing in the *tomboi* subject position because she considered same-sex behaviors to violate *adat*—a Muslim woman should not have any sexual thoughts about anyone except her husband. Subjected to this contradiction, Eddy improvised a strategy: she would invest in a *tomboi* identity without acting on it, that is, she would obtain pleasure by spending time with a woman, someone who was also attracted to her, but at the same time, refrain from performing the role of a *tomboi*, who is expected to initiate intimate behavior.

The narratives of these four *tomboi* demonstrate how they are prompted to reassess their sexuality after experiencing a new sexual discourse and romantic relationship in the training centers. The women recalled many of their past experiences, including childhood crushes, relationships with husband or boyfriends, and sexual reactions to make sense of their new experiences and practices at the training centers. At the same time, their new experiences also reshaped their past experiences. Migration constitutes a new opportunity for these women because it opens a new space for them to detach from previous heterosexual relationships and invest in interrelationships with women. *Tomboi* do not just passively sit and think about their identity. Rather, they need to establish interrelations with others—intersubjectivity—and be positioned as *tomboi* by their object of desire. *Tomboi* are encouraged to put forth effort, such as initiating physical contact and creating romantic surprises for their girlfriends. The pleasure they obtain from a same-sex relationship motivates them to identify themselves as a *tomboi*.

Evaluating the Attributes of Biological Men

The Indonesian women in this study come from a heterosexual background, meaning that they had a boyfriend or husband in Indonesia and later developed same-sex relationships with other Indonesian women in Hong Kong. Even though a few *tomboi* (like those in the previous section) had been aware of their feelings for women since childhood, they still considered dating men and getting married to be normal, even inevitable, as those around them were doing the same thing. Therefore, it is important to examine the construction of masculine attributes in the narratives of these Indonesian women, which in turn enable them to detach themselves from their previous heterosexual relationship and explore further possibilities of establishing romantic relationships with women.

Men are almost absent from the Indonesian migrant community. According to a research report issued by the Legislative Council Secretariat (2017a), 99 percent of migrant domestic workers in Hong Kong are women. There is little demand for Indonesian men to work for Hong Kong families since women, not men, are deemed to be ideal housekeepers. Unlike South Korea or Malaysia importing a steady number of Indonesian men to work in factories or the fishing industry, Hong Kong does not need male workers from developing countries because the factories in Hong Kong moved to mainland China when the opening policy took effect in the 1980s. In addition, immigration policy clearly states that migrant domestic workers in Hong Kong are not allowed to bring their husband or children to Hong Kong. Despite their absence in the migrant community, men were still mentioned in these women's narratives. Two main types of men were often discussed: (1) their boyfriend or husband in Indonesia and (2) South Asian men in Hong Kong.

Infidelity

Regardless whether they were married, the Indonesian women in this study were familiar with stories about men finding another woman when their wife or girlfriend was away from home to work in a foreign country. The stories may have been a first-person account or told by their girlfriend or friends. The women depicted these men as egoistic and selfish: they find another woman when their wife is working in Hong Kong or they gamble away the remitted funds from their wife intended for the family or children. Women, on the contrary, present themselves as caring and willing to sacrifice for the family. Among the fifteen married women in this study, eleven said that their goal of working overseas was to earn money for the family and their children. Only four of the married women said that they had their own agenda including escaping from a physically abusive husband, using overseas employment as an excuse to leave a forced marriage, and gaining overseas experience and earning large sums of money by working in Hong Kong. Although these four women left their husband for their own personal benefit instead of a more noble cause such as earning money for the family, they still shared the belief that that their husband was wrong for cheating on them while they are away. Two of the women in this study had a fiancé in Indonesia; both relationships could not survive long distance and fell apart. Both considered it the man's fault. One blamed her fiancé for sexual infidelity when she was away. The other accused her man of lacking integrity, as he kept asking her for money and lying that he used the money to fund his business in Jakarta; in fact, he gambled and drank all her money away.

I am not suggesting that there is a causal relationship between the men's infidelity or dishonesty and the change of the women's sexual preference. Instead, I examine how breaking up with men produced favorable conditions for these women to reconsider their sexuality when a woman approached them. The story of Jeni (twenty-eight years old) sheds light on the process of reconsidering sexuality:

> A woman became fond of me when I was still at the training center. But I did not respond to her love because I had a man in Indonesia. The man asked me to marry him and gave me a ring before I left. I accepted the ring and planned to return home and marry him after two years. So, at that time I didn't want to get involved with any woman. When I was in Hong Kong for the first two years, he kept asking me for money. I gave him money three times a year. By the end of my contract, he asked me to go back and marry him. I wanted to test him, so I said that I had to work in Hong Kong for one more year. If he was good during that one year, I would go back; if not, I wouldn't marry him. Then he asked me for HKD 3,000 [approx. USD 380]. I gave the money to him and expected that he would use the money to fund his business in Jakarta. But he didn't. He used the money for fun and gambling. At the time, I was in between a new and old contract and was staying in a boarding house provided by the employment agency. I ran into the woman who was fond of me at the training center. We began to hang out and stayed in the same boarding house as she was also waiting for a new contract. Whenever I talked to my man on the phone, I put it on speaker phone and let her listen in. She said, "You know the man is no good, why are you still with him and forsaking me?" I told her that I would give him one more year. During that year, I was already in a relationship with the woman but still thinking about getting married to a man. But after a whole year, I knew that the man is no good. So, I decided to stay with the woman.

After another year, Jeni parted ways with the woman. However, instead of reverting to heterosexual relationships, she had another same-sex relationship in Hong Kong. When I interviewed her, she had been in a relationship with a woman for seven months. She showed me a ring on her fourth finger and said while beaming, "It's from her."

Similar stories about the misconduct of Indonesian men circulate widely in the migrant community. These stories reinforce the sexual ideology that men are unreliable and unfaithful to their spouse. This produced a favorable condition for these women to detach from their previous relationships with men and explore different possibilities with women.

Skepticism about men

The comparative advantage of working as a migrant domestic worker in Hong Kong is that their monthly income falls into the middle-class range in Indonesia. The minimum allowable monthly wage of a migrant domestic worker in Hong Kong since October 2018 has been HKD 4,520, which is approximately 8.2 million rupiah or USD 578 (Government of the Hong Kong Special Administrative Region 2019). According to a survey of Indonesian consumers by Deloitte Consulting Southeast Asia, households making 5 million rupiah or more are considered upper-middle class, and they can spend their income extravagantly (*Nikkei Asian Review* 2015).

Migrant domestic workers' high income in Hong Kong seriously contradicts their perceived low status in Indonesia. The social status of migrant domestic workers in Indonesia is low because first, Indonesians regard domestic work as a low-status job (Elmhirst 2007). Second, migrant domestic workers usually come from rural areas and have only a junior high education. More than half, or 54 percent, of the women in this study have a junior high education, 40 percent have a high school education, and 6 percent only a primary school education. Third, the sexual purity of migrant domestic workers is questioned by the people in their village, who spread gossip about their sexual morality and possible engagement in sex work for quick money (Chan 2016). Therefore, the social status of migrant domestic workers is low even though their income is middle class.

The contradiction between their social status and financial means inadvertently influences how the unmarried women in this study perceive their potential spouse in Indonesia. When I asked about their expectations for a future spouse, the unmarried women wanted a hardworking man with a stable job. None mentioned his class background or that he should be rich. Being a hard worker is the most important attribute to these migrant women. This expectation shows that these women already assume that their future spouse will be an average man, probably from their own village, whose income would be far below theirs. They are aware that their social status does not enable them to marry a man from the middle class or one who lives in a large city.

Their high income but low social status provoked mixed feelings when the migrant women talked about their future spouse. On the one hand, they were aware that many Indonesian men are interested in having a migrant domestic worker as a girlfriend. On the other hand, they were skeptical about the intentions of these men, whose income was far less than theirs, and particularly those who did not mind their status as a migrant domestic worker and were eager to start a relationship with them. The following views shared by these Indonesian women will show why they have such a skeptical attitude toward Indonesian men.

Leo (thirty years old, unmarried) is a *tomboi*. She told me that she was returning to Indonesia when her contract ended next year. She decided not to pursue any relationships with women after returning home. She also shared her thoughts on developing relationships with men. In her remaining days in Hong Kong, she grew her hair longer to appear more feminine. She posted feminine-looking pictures of herself on Facebook, and she was approached by men. She shared with me one of her online experiences with an Indonesian man:

> I met a man on Facebook. Soon afterwards, he told me he loves me. We've never met in person. Just see each other's pictures. Why would he love me in a short period of time? So, I don't trust him.

Apart from first-person experience, a common belief that circulated in the migrant community is that Indonesian men like to date migrant domestic workers because they make a substantial income. Beby (twenty-four years old) did not have a boyfriend yet but told me in a confident tone, "There are many men who want us. They think we're very rich." Rachael (twenty-six years old) had a boyfriend but broke up when she went to work in Hong Kong. She said, "Indonesian men like rich women. They like us because we work overseas. They say they love you but after taking your things [money], they say bye-bye to you."

The huge income gap between these migrant women and the men in their hometown inadvertently produced an ambivalent feeling among the unmarried women, who have become skeptical about men, especially those who are too quick to show their affection. The popularity of online dating through Facebook also further increased their feelings of uncertainty about having a relationship with men.

South Asian men

Both the work conducted by Nicole Constable (2014) and by Gordon Mathews (2011) documented sexual relationships between Indonesian migrant women and South Asian men. The relationships ranged from dating, to sexual transactions, to stable relationships. However, the dance group members in this study disapproved of the South Asian men and believed that proper Indonesian women should not date them. In the following, I will first examine how race, gender, and sexuality shape the use of space in the parks by South Asian men and Indonesian women and, second, their impact on how these Indonesian women think of South Asian men.

At the main entrance of Victoria Park (facing the side of Causeway Bay) on Sundays, there are always South Asian men trying to catch the attention of Indonesian women. Whenever Indonesian women passed by, I saw them look at the women and say "Assalamualaikum" to them. This is an Arabic greeting commonly used by Muslims, meaning "may peace be upon you." Although eager to be friends, I never saw any South Asian men going into the park and approaching Indonesian women. In this sense, the space of Victoria Park is clearly marked by boundaries of race, gender, and sexuality. The South Asian men do not dare to cross its boundaries or enter the all-women areas. They just stand outside to lure a potential partner. The implication of the space allocation is obvious; the South Asian men gather around the park entrance with a clear purpose and act it out—greet the women who walk by and look for those who might be interested in them.

The scene in Kowloon Park is slightly different, and the spatial boundaries between Indonesian women and South Asian men are not as clearly marked as they are in Victoria Park. First, the number of Indonesian women on Sundays is far lower at Kowloon Park, which is too small for an all-women scene like the one in Victoria Park. Second, there is a mosque next to Kowloon Park, so it is common to see three to four South Asian men in a group walking through the park or sitting on the benches to rest and chat. There are also Hong Kong families and tourists who use the park. Therefore, Kowloon Park visitors are more diverse than those in Victoria Park.

I observed how South Asian men approached Indonesian women during a fashion show hosted by Champion on a Sunday afternoon in Kowloon Park. The fashion show was a simple and modest one without a stage or sound system. The judges sat on the ground when the contestants were walking the catwalk. Despite the limited decorations and equipment, the event still successfully attracted the attention of many passers-by, both men and women, of different ages and ethnicities. Four South Asian men sat on a bench very close to the two judges and the contestants. Unlike the other passers-by, who just watched for a while and then left, these four men sat down and enjoyed the show. One filmed the show with his cell phone. After Alexis (twenty-eight years old, *cewek*) finished her catwalk, they cheered and commented loudly, "This one is number 1!" They repeated this several times. Obviously, they wanted to draw her attention. However, Alexis did not respond to them, although her facial expression showed that she recognized their praise.

Since Champion met at the same spot in Kowloon Park for their gatherings, the members noticed the South Asian men who lingered around them. For instance, on a late Sunday afternoon, a few members of Champion were giggling about a young Indonesian woman who had done something very silly for her Pakistani boyfriend. The Indonesian woman did not know anyone in Champion, but she approached them and asked whether she could borrow the guitar one of the members was carrying. The member knew that the request was made on behalf of her Pakistani boyfriend who wanted to play the guitar. Therefore, the Champion members turned her down. Then the Indonesian woman said, "I beg you for it." They thought that the woman was very silly for begging them for the guitar to please her boyfriend. After she left, they told me that they had already recognized this Pakistani man, who always spent his Sundays sitting next to a fountain in the proximity of the Champion gatherings.

The above scenarios indicate that the members of Champion avoid contact with South Asian men in Hong Kong. Their negative impression of South Asian men as men who take advantage of Indonesian women is based on their everyday experiences, particularly their observations of the behavior of the South Asian men in the parks.

Apart from their observations, the women in this study were also familiar with stories of relationships between Indonesian women and South Asian men that resulted in unwanted pregnancies, abortions, or abandonment. The pop dance group members considered South Asian men in Hong Kong irresponsible and believed they would abandon a pregnant girlfriend. Sarah (twenty-six years old), the leader of another pop dance group, had worked in Hong Kong for seven years and two years in Taiwan before that. She told me her thoughts about South Asian men in Hong Kong:

> I have heard many stories when the Indonesian woman got pregnant and the man left her, like the Pakistani men here. When the woman goes home with the baby, people would say, "She goes to work and returns with no money but something else."

Sarah did not explicitly define the "something else" but giggled instead. She then went on to say, "There are many women who end up like that."

The other pop dance group members also said that they had heard about this predicament between Indonesian women and South Asian men. However, when I asked whether they knew a woman who had been abandoned by a South Asian man, none could provide any concrete details but just generalized.

This stereotype of South Asian men made the women in pop dance groups cautious when approached by South Asian men in public places. I asked Ria (twenty years old) whether any South Asian men ever talked to her. Ria made a disapproving face and said that they come to say hello to her when she is alone. I found Ria's experience to be common among the dance group members who have long hair and feminine style.

From the women's own observation of South Asian men to the anonymous stories about South Asian men who left Indonesian girls, the women in my study had come to hold a very negative impression of South Asian men. They believed that proper women should avoid South Asian men and not even to respond to their Islamic greeting. Even although Indonesian migrant workers could easily meet South Asian men, they found it difficult to trust them.

Hong Kong men

The category of Hong Kong men does not come up when Indonesian women talk about their former or future relationships with men. It only came up when I asked them whether they liked Hong Kong and want to stay further. Three women in this study mentioned the idea of becoming Hong Kong residents. They noted that marrying a Hong Kong man is a feasible way to obtain residency. Eva (*tomboi*, thirty years old, unmarried) had been working in Hong Kong for seven years. She had a long-term rental room of her own. She bought many electrical appliances, such as a refrigerator, a space cooler, a TV set, and the like. She also decorated to make her rental room as cozy as possible, with patterned curtains and framed photos of her girlfriend. She said she liked life in Hong Kong and wanted to stay permanently:

> I want to live in Hong Kong. But if I don't get married to a man here, I can't live here. I know there are people [women who want to become Hong Kong residents] paying a man, and then getting married with him.

I was surprised when Eva brought up bogus marriages because she was the only woman in this study who mentioned it. Eva had no interest in men; therefore, she could not imagine herself having a real marriage with a man at all. A bogus marriage seemed to be an option for her. I casually replied that it might be expensive. My response drew Eva's interest as she followed up and asked how much it would be. I said I did not know exactly. With her eyes showing a bit of disappointment, she said, "I want it."

Two other women, both *cewek*, mentioned that they wanted to become Hong Kong residents and knew that they could achieve this goal by marrying a Hong Kong man. But they were not serious about the idea. They mentioned it as a possibility but did not show any eagerness to reach out Hong Kong men to find a spouse. The option of establishing a family in Indonesia was much more desirable than having a Hong Kong husband for the two *cewek*.

Desiring Same-Sex Relationships and *Tomboi*

Among the forty-three Indonesian women in this study, nineteen were not previously interested in women or had not imagined that they would fall in love with a woman but then later engaged in a relationship with a *tomboi*. When asked about their first impression of *tomboi* in Hong Kong, they shared the view that they felt strange (*aneh*) and some even harbored feelings of hatred (*benci*). Their bad impression of *tomboi* was due to the behaviors of the *tomboi* in Hong Kong, including smoking, bleaching their hair, and wearing baggy jeans and hip-hop clothes. They said that proper women should neither dress like that nor smoke. Some recalled that they had been approached by *tomboi* at the training centers. Nini (twenty-three, unmarried) recalled that a *tomboi* professed her love to her at the training center. She angrily responded, "I am normal! I don't like you!" However, not everyone became angry. Upik (twenty-three, unmarried) said that a *tomboi* asked her to be her girlfriend. She thought that the idea of becoming the girlfriend of a woman was very strange, and so she told the *tomboi*, "I don't want [to be your girlfriend], but I can call you older brother." Upik acknowledged the *tomboi*'s masculinity by calling her "older brother" but refused to be her girlfriend. When the women took part in the pop dance groups in Hong Kong, they began to change their perception of *tomboi* and later even engaged in romantic relationships with *tomboi*. In the following, I examine the meanings of same-sex relationships to the Indonesian women who had no previous interest in women. How did they make sense of their same-sex relationship in Hong Kong and find pleasure in them?

Same-sex relationships as desirable

On a Sunday just past Hari Raya Idul Fitri,[2] all the members of Champion gathered at Victoria Park. The park was much more crowded than usual. Perhaps many Indonesian migrant workers who did not frequent this park regularly came on that Sunday to celebrate the festival. The park was bustling with noise and excitement, as the women were happy to celebrate the Indonesian festival with other Indonesians in a place far away from home. Their respect for the festival was embodied in their clothing, as all of them dressed up on the day. The mother of Champion wore a *kebaya*, which is a traditional Javanese garment that women wear on special occasions. This was the first time that I saw a pop dance group member in a *kebaya*. The others also dressed up but did not wear traditional clothing. Over half of the *cewek* wore dresses; the *tomboi* wore shirts, and one wore a blazer.

The couples displayed their relationship status by wearing the same color or the same clothing without compromising their feminine or masculine attributes. For example, Rachael wore a women's black long-sleeve shirt that clearly showed off her curves; her *tomboi* lover also wore a black shirt but in a very different style. The *tomboi* did not button her shirt and wore a man's crewneck

---

2. Hari Raya Idul Fitri is a festival to mark the conclusion of Ramadan (the fasting month). Muslims spend the day with relatives and friends. In Hong Kong, Indonesian migrant workers pick a Sunday closest to the festival to celebrate.

tee underneath, disguising her curves. By wearing the same color or same style of clothing, couple relationships were clearly announced at the celebration. In other words, the festival provided them a platform to display their same-sex relationship.

The members arranged the food in the center on mats and everyone sat around it. After they prayed, they stood up and formed two circles. The mother and father and two older sisters, the secretary and treasurer, stood in the outer circle, while the other members stood in the inner circle. The ritual started when the first person in the inner circle greeted the mother and wished her good fortune. The mother gave her a red packet containing money, symbolizing good luck. Muslims in Indonesia use envelopes of various colors and not red packets to give money during the festival. The Indonesian women in my study adopted the Hong Kong Chinese custom of using red packets. After receiving a red packet, the person moved on to greet the father and wish her good fortune. The two circles continued to greet each other in this way until every member had received a red packet from the mother and father, respectively. Every member participated in this ritual. Although some members arrived too late to participate in the ritual, upon arrival they immediately approached the mother and father and gave their best wishes to the parents. Then the parents gave red packets to them.

In the celebration, same-sex relationships were explicitly displayed in a positive way. The same-sex relationship between the mother and her *tomboi* lover was affirmed and respected in the reciprocal ritual of exchanging wishes and red packets. The mother and father were deemed respected figures. Members showed their respect to the couple and acknowledged the mother-father relationship in the ritual. Besides, members who were in a same-sex relationship showed their relationship by wearing the same color or the same style of clothing. Subject to the favorable ideology toward same-sex relationships, any member of the pop dance group knew that she should respect those who are in a same-sex relationship even if she was not attracted to women *yet*.

There were other subtle interactions among the members that rendered same-sex relationships desirable. Members came to meet in the park supposedly to spend time together; however, they acted in pairs instead of as a group. I observed that the members always sat next to their lover; they followed their lover whenever the lover went to the restroom or to buy snacks. My ethnographic account in the following will illustrate how interactions between members made same-sex relationships become desirable in the group. On a Sunday afternoon in Victoria Park, Ria (twenty years old, *cewek*) and I were chatting with two other couples. We decided to buy something to eat and went together to a snack bar. As we arrived at the snack bar, I was aware that the six of us inadvertently split into three couples when we were standing in front of the menu and discussing our order. The two couples were in two pairs; Ria did not have a lover at the time, so she was left out and stood with me. I observed that the members prioritized their romantic relationship over the group relationship—one should be with her lover all the time, even at a group gathering. Those who did not have a lover yet, like Ria, felt left out. Although the members were in a group, interactions between individual members were heavily influenced by their romantic relationships. The effects of such interactions increased the desirability of same-sex relationships in the pop dance group. Anyone who did not have a lover would want to have one so that she would not feel left out.

Falling in love with *tomboi*

In the previous section, the construction of same-sex relationships as desirable in the pop dance group was discussed. In this section, I will examine how these women come to find a relationship with a *tomboi* desirable. How do they position themselves as *cewek*? How do they make sense of the *tomboi*'s masculinity?

In Indonesian society, self is a relational concept (Blackwood 2010). The value of the self is established by relationships with significant others and is contextually salient. The women in the pop dance group related to each other in kin terms. In addition to mother and father, brother and sister, couples used husband and wife to address each other. Both *tomboi* and *cewek* told me that only a relationship with a husband and a wife made sense to them. They used the concepts of *manja* (pampering someone) and *dimanja* (being pampered by someone) to mark the difference between husband and wife. They assumed that husbands should enjoy pampering their wife, while wives were supposed to be happy when pampered by their husband. The relationship between a wife and a husband was determined by the practice of pampering, not biological difference. A female-bodied person became a husband when her acts of pampering were accepted by her wife. It was therefore the practice of pampering that maintained the husband-wife relationship.

The meaning of pampering, shared by both *tomboi* and *cewek*, incorporated a wide range of gendered activities. *Tomboi* were supposed to act like gentlemen by picking up their girlfriend from home and escorting her back home on Sunday, paying for dates, and buying gifts for her. Moreover, *tomboi* were expected to be responsible for the physical comfort of *cewek* by finding seats for them on public transportation, offering their thigh as a place to rest in the park, and so on. *Tomboi* were expected to be tough and strong, like men in Indonesia, and should not need as much rest as *cewek* do. Moreover, *tomboi* should make public displays of affection. This is consistent with the Indonesian context where women should feel embarrassed about showing affection and desire in public (Brenner 2005). *Tomboi* feel masculine by being physically stronger and the financial provider when they fulfill the duty of pampering their girlfriend. At the same time, *cewek* feel feminine, by waiting for *tomboi* to take them out and escort them home, and being physically weaker, when they are pampered by their *tomboi* partners.

Michelle (thirty-two, unmarried), the mother of Champion, found *tomboi* attractive in Hong Kong. However, she did not deny her desire for men even though she was in a relationship with Eddy, the father of Champion:

> I started working in Hong Kong in 2005. I chatted online with guys [biological men] and had a boyfriend. He is an Indonesian. One time, I noticed something when we chatted through the web camera. Then I found out that he has a family. He has a wife and a son. I was heartbroken. After that, I decided not to meet any more guys on the Internet. This is the reason why I become a lesbian. Now I am a lesbian. I have somebody [Eddy] who is like a man [*seperti laki-laki*] to take care of me. I like it better this way.

On a Sunday evening, I took the train with Michelle and Eddy. The train was very crowded. We had to stand because no seats were available. When the train doors opened, Eddy suddenly moved to an empty seat after a passenger left. Eddy then waved to Michelle and offered the seat to her, which Michelle accepted. She then leaned her head on Eddy, who was standing and facing Michelle. The couple looked at each other and whispered sweetly as if they were lone travelers on the train.

Michelle made sense of her relationship with Eddy by positioning herself as a wife, who is cared for and pampered by a masculine figure. The masculine figure could be either a man or a person who behaves like a man. Eddy's pampering made Michelle feel feminine and enabled Michelle to make sense of her same-sex relationship. She found the masculine attributes of *tomboi* attractive.

While Michelle's story is more about her personal interaction with her *tomboi* lover, the following story of Ria (twenty years old, *cewek*) will provide a broader picture of how group interactions enabled Ria, who had no interest in women before, to position herself as a *cewek* and develop her affection for *tomboi*.

Two months after arriving in Hong Kong, Ria attended a dance class organized by Hong Kong people. She met an Indonesian *tomboi* who was also a migrant domestic worker in the class. The *tomboi* was the vice president of Champion. Recognizing that Ria had talent, she invited her to join Champion. Ria told me that she was hesitant about the invitation because the *tomboi* smoked and had bright blonde hair, the very epitome of the stereotypical *tomboi*, whose behavior and appearance she disliked very much. Nevertheless, Ria followed the *tomboi* to Kowloon Park and met Michelle, the mother of Champion. Ria enjoyed her time with Champion, not only dancing but also her relationship with other members in the group. She gradually changed her perceptions of *tomboi*: "The *tomboi* seemed to be naughty and not nice, but actually they are very nice people!"

In her fourth month in Champion, other members began to pay more attention to Ria, particularly her relationship with the *tomboi* in the group. On a Sunday evening, I invited Ria to have a quick meal with me before going home. While we were waiting for the food, Ria showed me a picture on her phone. There were two people in the picture: Ria and a *tomboi*, the vice president of

Champion. Both were standing and smiling into the camera. The *tomboi* had her arm around Ria's shoulder. Ria said that the *tomboi*'s girlfriend, who is also a member of Champion, saw this picture by chance when Ria was playing with her phone. The girlfriend was not happy about this picture and asked Ria when they took the picture. I jokingly said, "You upset her [the *tomboi*'s girlfriend]!" Ria was nervous about my comment and explained, "I have never thought about having a relationship with Cale [the *tomboi*] or falling in love with her. I just see her as a brother." Ria also revealed that she gave Cale a small gift, a stuffed duck, as a birthday present. Her girlfriend was not there when Ria presented the gift to Cale. Later, the girlfriend found out that the stuffed duck was from Ria. Ria said that the girlfriend used to be friendly to her; however, she thought that her attitude had changed, and she was now cold and unfriendly after she found out about the picture and the stuffed duck. Ria said that she was not guilty, as she never intended to steal Cale away from her girlfriend. Ria further elaborated on her experience in Champion:

> Since I am single, whenever I am close to a *tomboi* in Champion, people would think that I want to steal the *tomboi*. Whenever I put up a picture of me with a *tomboi* on my phone as the wallpaper, people ask me whether the *tomboi* is my partner. Then, I changed the picture to me with another *tomboi*. People ask me the same question again. I feel like people see me as a woman who casually dates around. But if I'm really in a relationship with a *tomboi*, people would not think of me like that. The girlfriends would not get jealous of me so quickly if I have a lover.

The jealousy and gossip in the dance group positioned Ria as a woman who desires *tomboi*. It motivated her to think of *tomboi* as potential partners. Ria gradually identified with this subject position after spending months in the group. She did not dislike *tomboi* anymore and began to think of relationship possibilities with one. She denied interest in Cale because Cale was like her brother, not because she was not interested in *tomboi*. Ria's response demonstrated how her subject position in Champion (positioned by the group members as a *cewek*) shaped her attitude and desires toward *tomboi*.

Developing Intimacy

Building an intimate relationship with only one day off per week is not easy. Ria (*cewek*, twenty years old) had a boyfriend in junior high school but broke up when she decided to work in Hong Kong. She did not want to keep the boy waiting so she chose to end the relationship. In Hong Kong, Ria had a relationship with a *tomboi*. She enjoyed the relationship a lot as she told me, "It's very nice! She cares about me. She is fond of me. Just nice!" I further asked her about any difference between having a relationship with the boy and her *tomboi* lover. Ria mentioned the difficulty of building trust:

> When I was in junior high school in Indonesia, we could meet every day. In Hong Kong, it's not all good. Trust [with the lover] is little. [Kalau di Indonesia, di SMP, bisa ketemu satiap hari. Di Hong Kong, tidak semua baik. Percayaan is little.]

Apart from Sunday, the Indonesian women in this study rarely had a chance to meet their girlfriend on weekdays. The couples did not live close. None was living in the same residential compound. Therefore, they could not meet up in the market or other places when running errands. Hong Kong employers seldom allow their domestic workers to leave home during weekdays except to run errands for the household. The mind-set of Hong Kong employers is that daytime is working time, and so no personal time should be given. They allow rest time, but only at home. It is very hard for migrant domestic workers to steal time to meet their lover during the day. According to the Indonesian women, they serve two main types of households: the nuclear family with small kids, and the elderly. For the first type of family, the domestic worker usually has a packed schedule from day to night because she needs to take care of the kids in daytime and then prepare dinner before the parents come home from work. The domestic worker cannot steal time to meet up with anyone. For the second type of household, taking care of elderly is less demanding because the main duty is to prepare three meals a day and accompany the client to the park or to the clinic, and so on. Though the work is less tiring and allows more rest during the day, the domestic worker still cannot steal time to meet up with anyone because their employer is too old or weak to leave home on their own and is there to "watch" them the whole day.

Phone calls and text messages become major ways for couples to communicate. Only a few employers allow their worker to talk on the phone during the day. Therefore, Indonesian women mostly rely on text messages. Rachel was one of the few lucky ones allowed to make phone calls during the day. She called her *tomboi* lover every day. The couple had been together for a year. Rachel told me:

> We are on the phone for twenty-four hours. When one battery went out, I changed another one. We never leave our phone aside, even when we sleep.

Rachel spent HKD 300 (approx. 8 percent of her monthly salary) per month for phone cards. I asked Rachel why her employer allowed her to talk on the phone throughout the day. She explained:

> We are smart. Whenever my boss [the wife] comes to me, I whisper "My boss's coming, quiet." Then we stop talking. Once my boss is away, we start talking again. We talk very softly when the boss is at home. My boss knows that I am using a handsfree. She can see it because I tie up my hair when working. She's okay that I talk on the phone while working.

Jason, her *tomboi* lover, was less fortunate. She said:

I sleep in the living room, so even I make a phone call after work at night, I still talk very softly. The apartment is very small. My boss always nags at me when she hears me talking on the phone.

Some women have their own bedroom they can return to around 9 p.m. They can call their girlfriend and talk more freely. But sometimes it becomes a source of conflict if one has a packed daily schedule, but the other does not. Andri (twenty-seven years old) worked for a family of four with two small kids. She said she worked till 12 at night. Compared to her girlfriend, who worked for a family of three without small kids, Andri found her work very tiring, as she needed to bathe two kids after dinner, which took her a lot of time. She told me, "Sometimes my girlfriend called at night, but my work is not done yet. I just told her we talk later."

There are other ways to develop intimacy. Taking a stuffed animal or a doll as their own "child" is common among the couples. Ria and her *tomboi* lover had a stuffed duck. She showed me a 2R-size picture of her with her *tomboi* lover and a stuffed yellow duck. The couple stood close and held the stuffed duck in front of their chests together. Ria pointed at the stuffed duck and said, "This is our child." Another couple, Rachel and Jason, had a stuffed monkey. I saw the stuffed monkey on the day I conducted an in-depth interview with Rachel and Jason at Victoria Park. Rachel held the stuffed monkey all the time. I guessed the stuffed monkey was their "child," so I asked Rachel its name. The couple looked very sweet when they heard my question. Rachel said:

> We got him from Ocean Park. His name is Marky. Jason's idol is Mark of Westlife; this is a monkey, so we have the name Marky. We went to Ocean Park on our wedding day[3] and we got Marky.

A few days later, Rachel sent out a SMS message to all members of Champions. In the message, she drew a house and invited people to come to dance. The message was not really an invitation to her house but to initiate conversations with members on weekdays. Below was my SMS correspondence with Rachel about her "child":

> Francisca: Is Marky at home? Say hello to Marky. [Marky ada drmhnya? Salam buat Marky.]
>
> Rachel: Marky is bathing. Do you know Marky is very naughty? When I am taking a shower for him, he sprays water to my face. [Marky sedang mandi. Hehehe do you know he very naughty. When I shower for him, he spry water to my face.]
>
> Francisca: Marky is naughty. [Marky nakal.]
>
> Rachel: Hahaha, but his father is naughtier! [Hahaha tp bapaknya lebih nakal wo.]

---

3. Rachel and Jason did not officially get married. They took the first day of their relationship as their wedding day.

Rachel called Jason "the father" (*bapaknya*), and she took on a mother's role to bathe Marky. These stuffed animals are not just toys. Couples project a familial relationship onto the stuffed animal, which becomes a meaningful medium for the couples to express their affection and attachment when they cannot meet during the week.

A few couples told me that they go to rental rooms if they want to make love. They said they would spend half a day there, usually from 10 a.m. to 4 p.m. The price was around HKD 200 (approx. USD 25) for six hours. I did not ask further about their sexual practices, but from the number of hours they spent in the room, it seems that they did not use it only as a place for making love but also for rest. Since I did not have a chance to go to the kind of rental rooms that they went to, I cannot provide any more details here.

Gender Shifting between *Tomboi* and *Cewek*

The kin world subjects every individual to either a *tomboi* or *cewek* position. Nevertheless, it is erroneous to assume *tomboi* or *cewek* to be rigid, static categories. In the Indonesian migrant community, it is not uncommon to see two individuals in a romantic relationship shift between the positions of *tomboi* and *cewek*. I will proceed to discuss the practice of shifting gender and its implications for understanding the fluidity of the gender system and formation of sexual subjectivity in the pop dance groups.

Sarah (twenty-six, *cewek*, engaged) and Rachael (twenty-six, *cewek*, unmarried) looked feminine to me. Both had shoulder-length hair; both had a *tomboi* lover. When I conducted an in-depth interview with each of them, I was told that they were *tomboi* in the past. Based on their appearance and relationship status, I had no idea about their gender change before their confession during the interviews. Both Sarah and Rachael told me that they became *tomboi* because they were heartbroken after their *tomboi* lover left them. When they transformed into *tomboi*, they changed their object of desire from *tomboi* to *cewek*, in addition to wearing young men's clothing and hairstyle.

As a *tomboi*, Sarah fulfilled the responsibility of pampering her girlfriend. Sarah said, "When I was a *tomboi*, I wore very different clothing. Then I got myself a girlfriend. I paid whenever we ate out. If she used up her phone card, I refilled it for her." Though *tomboi* are expected to do things for their girlfriend, they have some rights that *cewek* are not entitled to—chasing girls. Sarah continued, "I looked cool when I was a *tomboi*. I chased girls." Rachael also had relationships with *cewek* after becoming a *tomboi*. Rachael sounded proud when she recalled how handsome she looked and her past relationships with *cewek*. Rachael said, "After I cut my hair short, many girls were attracted to me. . . . That was the first time that I became naughty. Four months, three *cewek*." Therefore, shifting to the position of *tomboi* includes changing both appearance and object of desire.

Gender is fluid. Sarah, Rachael, and two other *cewek*, April and Nini, became *cewek* again when their new *tomboi* lover asked them to do so. They grew their hair long and wore women's styles, such as dresses or pink clothing. Both April and Nini were teased by their friends when they became *cewek* again. April (twenty-six, unmarried) told me:

> At the time, my hair was short, so I wore a wig on my days off. My friends laughed at me and said that I was a *waria*.[4] They said that I didn't walk like a girl and still looked like a boy.

April considered shoulder-length long hair to be symbolic of femininity; therefore, she wore a wig to emphasize her *cewek* identity. However, her friends thought that the wig was artificial femininity. Therefore, they teased April by calling her a *waria*.

Nini (twenty-three, unmarried) shared a similar experience. She told me in her interview, "When I was changing from *tomboi* to feminine, I began to wear dresses again. But in the beginning, I felt strange about wearing a dress. The funniest thing is that sometimes I forgot that I was wearing a dress and I spread my legs open when I was sitting in Victoria Park. I didn't realize it until my friends laughed at me!"

April and Nini did not take the comments from their friends negatively. Rather, they took the comments as a kind of motivation to work on their hairstyle, clothes, and mannerisms. Teasing should not be considered as punishment for or disapproval of the change in gender. Rather, the teasing serves as constructive comments to improve their appearance and gestures to be consistent with the current gender identity.

These stories show that the gender system in the pop dance groups allows individuals to shift between the two genders as long as their newly changed identity, appearance, and object of desire are coherent. By coherent, I refer to the notion of "matrix of intelligibility" used by Judith Butler (1999, 24). Butler noted that intelligible genders are those that maintain relations of coherence and continuity among sex, gender, and desire. After shifting to the opposite gender, these women maintain coherent relations by changing their gender appearance and object of desire accordingly. I argue that sex, gender, and desire are not necessarily equally weighted in the matrix of intelligibility. The migrant community values gender and desire differently. Desire, that is, the intelligibility of same-sex relationships, is more valuable than gender identity. A relationship between two *cewek* or two *tomboi* is not considered intelligible by the community because

---

4. *Waria* is an Indonesian term for transgender women, who are biologically men and identify as women. The word *waria* is made up by two words, *wanita* (an Indonesian word for "women") and *pria* (an Indonesian word for "men").

two *cewek* or two *tomboi* do not fit the husband-wife model. It would seriously disturb the kin world and kin relations. Gender identity is less valued; therefore, it is acceptable for one of the two to change to the opposite gender to maintain the intelligibility of a same-sex relationship.

I also argue that the notion of coherence should be contextualized in the kin world because the seemingly incoherent practice of gender shifting makes the same-sex relationship coherent with the kin relations: mother and father, wife and husband. Rather than viewing gender and sexual subjectivity as mere personal identification markers, the kin world is shown to have significant impacts on sexual subject formation.

What makes the shift desirable? The theory of the subject in Moore can perhaps offer an answer. Moore proposed the notion of "intersubjectivity" to analyze how individuals take up positions that are outside the culturally defined model. Moore argues that "one's interrelations with other individuals will determine what positions one takes up" (1994, 65). Individuals need others to recognize their position and, at the same time, are concerned with how others position them. Therefore, the four women were motivated to adopt the position of the opposite gender through interrelations with their new lover. When their new *tomboi* lover positioned them as *cewek* and asked them to change from *tomboi* to *cewek*, they began to evaluate the change based on the satisfaction received from the relationship. April explained:

> If I really love someone, I would change for that person. . . . Actually, I like to be pretty, and be a girl. I am a girl. But later if I meet someone and she wants me to be a *tomboi*, I think I would change for her if I really love her.

Sexual subjectivities are formed through negotiation: who becomes the husband and who becomes the wife. The negotiation aims to ensure that the couple has different genders, so that the relationship is intelligible.

Summary

This chapter has shown that the Indonesian women have different evaluations and expectations of men and *tomboi*, respectively. Although *tomboi* share some features of masculinity possessed by men, such as the privilege of chasing girls and the expectation of pampering their girlfriend, *tomboi* are perceived as better lovers than men in this context. The women have little trust of Indonesian men because of the long distance and huge income gap. While South Asian men are here and have similar income, they see them as dangerous and lacking integrity because they think they would abandon a pregnant girlfriend. They regard same-sex relationships as safer, more trusting, and more desirable than heterosexual relationships. The religious factor will be discussed in the next chapter. Therefore, it is erroneous to assume that these women cannot find a man in Hong

Kong and so they turn to a same-sex relationship. Indeed, they can find a man easily but choose not to partner with one because of racial prejudice and lack of trust. The discourse about men serves as an important background for understanding how the Indonesian women, who had no interest in women before, turn their desire toward women.

This chapter has also provided ethnographic details of the migrant community for contextualizing the women's gender and sexual subjectivities, including how they identify their gender position and find same-sex relationships desirable. Their gender and sexual preferences are not merely their personal identification or sexual orientation but the intersubjectivity among the pop dance group members. Their daily interactions in the kin world, the normalization of *tomboi* in the performance events, gossip about the women who date South Asian men, and the meanings and satisfaction obtained from their same-sex relationships all have significant impacts on how the Indonesian women frame the sexual subject. It is also noteworthy that their new experiences of same-sex intimacy simultaneously reshape their past experiences and relationship with their husband or boyfriend in Indonesia. Labor migration has offered a new space and time for the women to reconsider their sexuality, intimacy, and pleasure.

3
Negotiating Social Positions

Religion, Class, and Race

The intersectionality of religion, class, and race on the formation of the gender and sexual subjectivities of Indonesian migrant women in Hong Kong is examined in this chapter. The different identities (Muslim, live-in maid, Indonesian, wife, mother, and lesbian) do not stand alone. Instead, these seemingly conflicting identities intersect and intertwine with each other.

The first issue that this chapter will address is the conflict between the Islamic identity and a lesbian identity. As noted by Constable (2011), labor migration provides space and freedom as well as distance from religion. At the beginning, the break from religious expectations might be involuntary. There are cases in which employers force their Indonesian worker to consume pork or ban their praying. The religious subjectivity of the migrant women, such as their attitudes toward religious decrees and piety, gradually changes when they are distanced from their religion for a long time. The disentanglement from religious rules gradually serves as an excuse to explore practices that are inconceivable in Indonesia. Therefore, in this chapter, the changing and negotiable definitions of religious piety are explored, and how these migrant women reconcile their lesbian desires with Islamic principles is examined. By situating the reconciliation process in the migratory process, I track the practices of the Indonesian government, employment agents, and the parents of these Indonesian women and consider how their practices changed the women's views of religion and piety. This will lead to a better understanding of how these Indonesian women reconciled the assumed conflicts between their religious identity and same-sex relationships in Hong Kong.

The second question that will be addressed in this chapter is about the intersectionality of race, class, gender, and sexuality. I examine how the rules, which are established by Hong Kong people, shape the discourse on the sexuality of Indonesian migrant women and how Indonesian women react to this discourse. Based on in-depth interviews with Indonesian women about their employer and my participant observation in karaoke boxes and rental rooms operated by Hong

Kong people, I situate the discussion in three specific contexts: (1) the home of the employer, (2) the karaoke boxes, and (3) monthly rental rooms (not the love hotels). The three contexts provide clarity on the rules established by Hong Kong people, as well as the interactions between Hong Kong people and Indonesian women. These Indonesian women do not necessarily conform to the rules but negotiate and reestablish their boundaries. I examine the effects of gendered expectations, particularly on producing a space that allows and even encourages women to wear masculine outfits and conduct same-sex relationships. Rather than assuming heteronormativity as a fixed set of expectations and behaviors, my work unravels the intertwined effects of race, class, and gender on shaping the sexual subjectivity of Indonesian women.

The Indonesian Government: Reconciling Islamic Expectations with Overseas Work

Orthodox Islam assumes that a woman is a dependent daughter prior to marriage. In the event that an unmarried woman must leave her residence, she is supposed to be accompanied by a male guardian (*wali*) (Bennett 2005). However, the immigration laws of Hong Kong and other host countries do not grant visas to the husband or relatives of migrant domestic workers. This means that Indonesian women must leave home without the protection of her male guardian. The Indonesian government has been able to reconcile this gendered expectation by emphasizing the safety of working overseas.

Having maintained that its female nationals would be safe in a devoutly Muslim country, so in the mid-1980s, the Indonesian government began to export female nationals to Saudi Arabia for employment purposes. As noted by Kathryn Robinson (2000), Indonesian women were enticed by not only higher earnings but also the opportunity of making the pilgrimage to Mecca. Lower-class women, especially those with little education in rural areas, jumped at the chance to work as a domestic worker in Saudi Arabia.

Nevertheless, the Indonesian press has reported maltreatment of Indonesian women by employers in Saudi Arabia since 1984. This caused a nationwide debate on whether Indonesia should stop sending women to work overseas.

However, the Indonesian government could not really stop sending female nationals to work overseas because it relied heavily on their remittances. Instead, the propaganda wheel portrayed the women as economic heroes (*pahlawan devisa*) who worked overseas and sent money back home (Elias 2013). Tacitly admitting to the abuse of the Indonesian women in Saudi Arabia, the Indonesian government solved the problem by diversifying work destinations to include cities in East Asia, such as Hong Kong, where the rights of migrant domestic workers are legally recognized, in addition to the higher income relative to Saudi Arabia (Anggraeni 2006; Wee and Sim 2005).

While diversifying work destinations appears reasonable because of superior legal protections available to Indonesian migrant workers, the Indonesian government neglected the issue of religion. In the past with Saudi Arabia, the Indonesian government was able to reconcile the Islamic expectation of the protection of a male guardian required outside the home with assuring women's safety by working in a devoutly Muslim country. However, this would not hold true anymore because Hong Kong has only a minority population of Chinese Muslims of 40,000 out of its 7 million residents (Legislative Council Secretariat 2017b). Besides, pork is a daily protein staple for most Hong Kong Chinese people. The Indonesian government strategically dodged the religious conflicts between the diet of Chinese families and that of Muslims by emphasizing the better legal protection and higher salary in the East Asian cities.

In the one-day predeparture briefing organized by the Indonesian government (as required by Law39/2004), prospective migrant workers are taught about "personality and spirituality," "working conditions," "HIV AIDS, sexual disease and trafficking," and "the work contract." In the "personality and spirituality" classes, Olivia Killias observed how instructors reinterpreted Islamic teachings to promote self-discipline and obedience to employers. The women workers were told that all kinds of work are equal, and so Allah would not mind what kind of work they do abroad (Killias 2018). While the government is keen on telling the women to be better workers and better Muslims, the religious conflicts between the diet of Chinese families and that of Muslims are not the concern of the government.

Employment Agents: Improvising Ways to Address Pork and Dogs

The previous literature has noted that spiritual education, that is, teaching women workers to be docile and obedient, is very important during the training period, apart from transferring work and language skills to them (Liang 2011; Robinson 2009). During their time at the training centers, the women workers are punished if they fail to obey rules. Employment agents prepare résumés for women workers that contain little information on their profession and skills and instead focus on their obedience and address the specific requests of employers, such as eating pork (Liang 2011). Paul O'Connor (2016) also observed that receptiveness to pork consumption is used as a selling point for Indonesian domestic workers in employment agency advertisements in Hong Kong. This shows that employment agents are fully aware of the requirement for Indonesian women workers to touch, cook, and consume pork and even care for dogs when they begin their work life in Hong Kong. After admitting Indonesian women to the training centers, how do employment agents reconcile Islamic expectations, which include no contact with pork or dogs, with the primary duties of domestic work for the Chinese families?

Learning how to reconcile the Islamic principles with the lifestyle of Chinese families is an important part of their spiritual education. Anggraeni (2006) briefly discussed how the training centers in Indonesia address the Islamic principles. For example, the cooking classes show the Muslim students how to handle pork without compromising their own religious observance as well as instructions on how to handle dogs. The trainers also inform the women workers that they should not wear a white prayer cape but a floral cape because white is a mourning color in Chinese culture. The movie *Minggu Pagi Di Victoria Park* (2010; *Sunday Morning in Victoria Park*) documented the main character, an Indonesian domestic worker working for a Chinese family in Hong Kong, wearing plastic gloves as a solution to preparing pork for her employer without compromising her Islamic observance. In her ethnographic study, Olivia Killias documented the advice given by the director of a training center whom the workers came to visit the night before leaving for Hong Kong. In addition to reminding the workers to pray two times a day, the director also mentioned eating pork to the workers: "Eating pork! You are smart enough, you know how to handle that, do you? If you want to eat it, eat it, if not, you don't have to" (2018, 137). The above examples show how the training centers improvise and teach the Indonesian women ways to handle conflicts between their domestic work responsibilities in Hong Kong and the Islamic rules.

Parents: "Allah Will Understand"

Parents also play a crucial role in the reconciliation process. Before Indonesian women leave for Hong Kong, their parents have already taken steps to remedy the possible violations of the Islamic rules resulting from the Chinese lifestyle. Ria (twenty years old, unmarried) said that her mother taught her how to care for dogs and touch pork without compromising her religious principles:

> My mother told me that I shouldn't touch dog saliva because it is very dirty to Muslims. She told me that it's fine to touch dog skin because it's my duty to take care of my employer's three dogs. But in case I touch dog saliva, she told me to use salt to rub and clean my hands ten times. It's the same if I touch pork. I have to clean my hands thoroughly.

Ria continued:

> But I feel like religion is far away since I began to work in Hong Kong. I touch pork every day; so, I decided not to pray or fast here. You know that I must rub my hands with salt ten times after touching pork. But I work here and touch pork and dogs every single day. So I think Allah would understand me why I don't pray or fast because I have to work here. My mother also said to me, "Allah will understand."

When other Indonesian women were asked about their feelings when they touch pork or dogs in Hong Kong, they shared Ria's view, although they did not mention using salt to clean themselves. These women generally felt reassured because their parents and other Indonesian Muslims in Hong Kong understood that their work duties were beyond their control. They emphasized that if they only touch pork but did not consume the meat, they were fine. They also mentioned that they would not touch pork or dogs anymore after they return to Indonesia. It is noteworthy that none of the Indonesian women in this study consulted the Qur'an or sought advice from a religious authority. They relied on the reassurance given by their parents and came to believe that "Allah will understand."

The boundary between acceptable and unacceptable violations of religious rules is blurry; for instance, why is it acceptable to touch dog skin but not dog saliva? Indeed, the boundary is set by the personal interpretations of the women and their parents. The level of concern over religious rule violation also varied among them. Some were much less concerned than Ria.

Justifying: "Only Here"

Following the claim that "Allah will understand," the women inadvertently separated the space of Hong Kong from that of their homeland. That is, Allah will understand and forgive their violation of religious rules because the offense took place only in the space of Hong Kong. This implies that if the same behavior were to take place in the space of Indonesia, Allah would not be so forgiving. The separation of space between Indonesia and Hong Kong therefore becomes essential to the reconciliation process. In this section, I discuss how these Indonesian women used the idea of *cuma di sini* (only here) to justify their same-sex relationships in Hong Kong, although the idea was originally used to alleviate the conflicting feelings about touching pork or dogs during their work in Hong Kong.

Most of the Indonesian women in this study considered their same-sex relationship to be a sinful behavior. When asked, they told me that they felt a conflict between their religion and lesbianism because Muslims do not allow women to be with women (*Muslim tidak boleh cewek sama cewek*). Sarah (twenty-six years old, engaged) said:

> Muslims are prohibited from doing that [having a same-sex relationship]. I know I shouldn't do it. What I'm doing now [having a same-sex relationship] is only here. I only do it here. Muslims don't do this kind of thing in Indonesia.

April (twenty-six years old, unmarried) used the word *nakal* (naughty) to describe her conflicting feelings about her same-sex relationship in Hong Kong:

Indonesians should pray but also need to be clean. They shouldn't have a romantic relationship with a girl [because it is unclean to do so]. I can't pray because I have a girlfriend. Since I don't pray, I'm *nakal* [naughty]. For me, having a girlfriend is in Hong Kong only. After I go home, I don't think so.

Sarah's and April's views are common to the Indonesian women in this study, both *tomboi* and *cewek*. Cale (twenty-eight years old, *tomboi*, unmarried) was aware of the conflict between Islam and lesbianism: "My religion does not allow it, but I don't care. . . . Later when I return to Indonesia, I don't think I will be with girls anymore." They considered their same-sex relationships wrong, and they also considered themselves religiously unclean. Even so, they did not refrain from taking a same-sex lover but emphasized that they did so only in Hong Kong.

The women also constructed their same-sex relationship as a primary source of emotional support in Hong Kong. Ria (twenty years old, unmarried) said:

I don't follow my religion here. I need somebody who is just like a husband to me. I want someone to love me and take care of me, so that I can be happy here.

By adopting the notion of *cuma di sini*, these women negotiated Islamic principles. That is, they rationalized their same-sex behavior by emphasizing the hardships and loneliness in Hong Kong. They claimed that having a lover could help them tolerate the situation. Otherwise, they could not stand the hardships here.

The notion of *cuma di sini* is at work when these women claimed that their same-sex relationship produced no actual consequences for their family honor in Indonesia. As shown in the previous section, these women perceived religion not only as a relationship between them and Allah but also as their family honor. This explains why they would agree to touch pork and take care of dogs when their mother reassured them that these behaviors were acceptable in Hong Kong. In the process of reconciling their lesbian behavior and Islamic principles, these women alleviated their sense of guilt and conflicting feelings because their family did not know about their lesbian behavior, which would not damage their family honor. The following story of Eddy (twenty-nine years old) sheds light on the reconciliation process.

Eddy was the father of Champion. She was not only responsible for teaching other *tomboi* to dance but also served as the prayer leader for Champion events and competitions. Her *tomboi* appearance and lesbian behavior did not undermine her religiosity in the group. When other Champion members wore a woman's headscarf on special occasions, Eddy used a man's bandanna to cover her hair but not her neck, as the *cewek* did. Eddy improvised ways to maintain her religiosity without compromising her *tomboi* identity. When I asked her how she handled the conflicts between Islam and her lesbian behavior, Eddy told me that it was not a big problem yet because she was still in Hong Kong. Her parents did not know much about her relationship with Michelle (the mother of Champion). Eddy explained to me, "My parents know that I am close to Michelle. But they think we're only best friends. They don't know that we kiss like a husband and a wife." Her narrative demonstrates how Indonesian women use the sentiment of *cuma di sini* (only here) to justify that their same-sex relationship as harmless to the family honor. It alleviates conflicting feelings between Islam and lesbianism, which allows them to continue their same-sex relationships in Hong Kong.

It is noteworthy that the notion of *cuma di sini* is not an excuse made up by these Indonesian women; it is formed at many points, including the policies and actions taken by the Indonesian government and employment agents as well as the reassurance given by parents, as shown above.

Islamic Piety of Pop Dance Groups

Islam emphasizes orthopraxy, that is, the rightness of actions and procedures. Muslims are required to pray five times a day (salat); however, Muslims in Hong Kong (both residents and migrant domestic workers) vary in their willingness and ability to do so. For instance, most Muslim youths in the study by O'Connor managed three prayers a day; some of the Muslim adults are infrequent prayers; and Indonesian migrant domestic workers could not manage daily prayers at all during their busy workday. O'Connor noted that although Islam emphasizes orthopraxy, not all Muslims worship regularly; instead, "many Muslims pray simply when they feel like it" (2012, 87).

Muslim women in Indonesia are not generally required to practice female seclusion, and the wearing of the *jilbab* is more a personal choice than a religious requirement (Bennett 2005). During the 1980s and 1990s, there was a rise of Islamic revivalism among middle-class, well-educated young people. Urban young women donned the *jilbab* as a sign of protest against the Suharto government (Brenner 1996). But this is not typically translated into the lives of rural people. In rural areas, only older women don the *jilbab* regularly (Jones 2007). The Indonesian women in this study, who grew up in rural areas in the 1980s and 1990s, recalled that they were not required to wear the *jilbab* except on the Islamic New Year or for special occasions. It was not until the spread of Islamic fundamentalism in the 2000s (the post-Suharto period) that Indonesian women began to don the *jilbab* regularly. The trend of wearing the *jilbab* also spread to the Indonesian migrant community in Hong Kong (Constable 2011).

Members of the pop dance groups neither prayed five times a day nor wore a *jilbab* and claimed that unclean women should not. They defined being unclean as touching pork or having a same-sex relationship. Although the women claimed that they were unclean, they had their ways of observing Islam during their Sunday activities.

Whenever there was a birthday party or a celebration, a prayer (*doa*) was said at the beginning, which usually lasted five to ten minutes. According to the Indonesian women in this study, everyone was welcome and could say a short prayer (*doa*) together. It is different from salat, which they considered to be more serious and prohibited unless a Muslim is clean.

The celebration could take place at either a karaoke box or in the park, depending on the financial resources of the organizer. An air-conditioned karaoke box is considered a decent place to host a birthday party. Although the venue is not religious at all, the women still would say a short prayer together. At the birthday party for Michelle (the mother of Champion), her *tomboi* lover, Eddy, served as the prayer leader. Eddy, Michelle, and the guests stood and formed a circle. A birthday cake, Indonesian food (the signature yellow rice in a cone shape with a whole chicken, satays, and vegetables), and drinks (nonalcoholic) were placed in the center of the table. Eddy held a wireless microphone, which was usually used for singing, and started the *doa*. Michelle and the guests closed their eyes with their palms gently bent and upward facing. However, not all the guests had the patience to pray. Cale amused her girlfriend by touching her girlfriend's chin. Both found it very enjoyable. Since they did not make any noise, the other guests, including Eddy and Michelle, were not bothered by Cale's playful behavior during the prayer.

The birthday party for Eddy, which was held half a year after Michelle's party, was more religious in terms of the clothing of the guests, duration of the prayer, and provision of prayer books to the guests. The birthday party was held in Victoria Park. Around fifteen Champion members attended. Everyone was in their usual clothing. When the *doa* was about to begin, everyone retrieved a headscarf from their bag to cover their hair and neck. Eddy did not don a woman's headscarf but used a man's white bandana to cover her hair. Eddy then distributed a prayer book to everyone and started to pray, for around ten minutes. Every member followed the prayer with the prayer book in their hands. When the prayer was finished, they took off their headscarf and reverted to their usual appearance.

Unlike Eddy, not all *tomboi* in Champion refused a women's headscarf during prayer. Joy (thirty-nine years old, married, mother of a son) identified herself as a *tomboi* and positioned herself as the husband in her relationship with Alexis (twenty-eight years old). At Eddy's birthday party, Joy donned on a women's headscarf for the prayer even though she was dressed in a *tomboi* style, with a men's plaid shirt and a pair of baggy jeans. At another religious occasion, Joy appeared in full female attire. This was the opening ceremony of Champion's annual anniversary event, in which Joy served as the *doa* leader. She wore a set of brown Islamic clothing, which had long sleeves that covered her arms and legs, along with a black headscarf with shoulder-length white, gauzy fabric on top. Her shoes were also women shoes, with a yellow ribbon on the toe cap. It was the first time that I had ever seen Joy in a full set of women's clothing. Once the prayer was done, Joy returned backstage. When she appeared on stage again, she was in a men's black jumpsuit. When the MC announced the names of the awardees in the *tomboi* fashion show, one of the awardees did not appear. After waiting a while, Joy went up to the stage to represent the missing *tomboi*, so that the show could move on without further delay. Her impromptu appearance on the stage fully reflected her *tomboi* identity.

The *tomboi* did not position themselves as men when praying. They did not occupy a separate space; both *tomboi* and *cewek* formed a circle together when praying. In Islam, men and women are separated during prayer. If there is only one prayer room, men occupy the front part of the room, and women the back. The only difference I observed between *tomboi* and *cewek* is that some *tomboi*, like Eddy, did not don a women's headscarf during praying.

During Ramadan (the fasting month), the members of Champion held their weekly gathering as usual. They did not abstain from food or drink in the daytime.[1] One member mentioned to me that her employer did not want her to fast. She did not insist, as her household duty was heavy. The situation in Hong Kong was very different from her experience in Indonesia. During Ramadan in Indonesia, she fasted and avoided hard work to save energy in the daytime. In Hong Kong, she could not avoid any duty at all. Although the members of Champion did not fast during Ramadan, they celebrated Hari Raya Idul Fitri, a festival that marks the conclusion of Ramadan. I described their celebration of Hari Raya Idul Fitri in Chapter 2.

Although the dance group members did not follow every religious rule, such as praying five times a day or fasting during Ramadan, they were religious. They observed Islam during their Sunday gatherings and had their own ways to express their piety. Their Islamic identity had not been forgotten at all.

A New Interpretation of Islamic Faith

Five of the Indonesian women in this study had a more critical view of the perceived conflicts between Islam and lesbianism. They were affirmed in their same-sex desire and reconciled their inner conflict by reinterpreting their religious principles. Although the views of these five women were not dominant in the migrant community, their process of reconciling Islam and lesbianism sheds light on the agency and religious subjectivity of these migrant women. The following narratives demonstrate that their faith in Islam does not necessarily prevent them from having a same-sex relationship but instead gives them strength to reconcile their same-sex relationship with their faith.

---

1. During Ramadan, Muslims are expected to abstain from food or drink after sunrise and before sunset. They can eat and drink at nighttime.

Islam appears to subject women to a passive position. However, some Indonesian women have transformed religious passivity into strength and use this strength to reconcile their inner conflict during the migration journey. As noted by Loïs Bastide, Muslim migrant women from Indonesia are inspired to work overseas but are also aware of the risks of the journey. However, they interpret the overseas journey as a religious trial. They demonstrate their agency by convincing themselves they should accept the challenge given by Allah. They use faith to support their decision to work overseas. The analysis in Bastide (2015) of agency and faith is useful for examining how the Indonesian women in this study use their faith to reconcile the conflicting feelings caused by their same-sex relationship.

For Yanis (twenty-seven years old, married), her faith in Islam had little to do with Islamic principles. Yanis was aware of the many religious rules that she was supposed to follow. However, she broke one of them when her first employer offered her no food other than pork. She was only twenty years old at the time. She did not dare refuse the food offered as it might upset her employer. Therefore, she ate the pork. This involuntary violation of religious principles provided a window for Yanis to revisit the taboo of eating pork:

> My Cantonese was very bad at the time. Besides, I feared my employer. So, I didn't tell them Muslims don't take pork. I told myself that eating pork is fine because it is already a blessing to have food. Then, I began to ask myself why Muslims don't eat pork because pork is just another type of meat. Now, I don't feel conflicted about eating pork. Pork tastes quite good actually. My favorite dish is Chinese barbeque pork. Very delicious!

Yanis further shared her views on Islamic principles:

> This religion has a lot of rules, so you can't do this and can't do that. If I follow all the rules so that I am a proper Muslim, I don't think I would be happy. I don't care about the principles. I follow my heart and do things that would make me happy. Muslims should not have same-sex relationships, but I have one anyway.

I asked Yanis whether she prayed salat daily. She said:

> Sometimes I pray. If time allows, I wear a full veil to pray. When I feel confused and don't have anyone to talk to, I will pray. It makes me feel calm. When I pray, I feel that someone is listening to me. My dad passed away, so I need to do more prayers for him. I pray but I don't do it regularly. Sometimes I do it once a week, sometimes once a month.

Since Yanis ate pork, I asked her whether she would avoid pork on the day that she was going to pray. She said:

> It's not like that. Salat is about your heart and feelings. I won't avoid eating or touching anything because I am going to pray.

Yanis's narrative shows the transformation of her religious principles, which started with an involuntary violation of eating pork at her employer's home. In the interview, Yanis also mentioned her trials during the migration journey, including her husband's affairs and being underpaid and deprived of a day of rest by her former employer. She felt the need to pray when helpless and lonely. While Yanis put her faith in Allah, she reflected on religious principles and piety as well. She differentiated herself from other Muslims, who strictly followed the rules; she ate pork and was involved in a same-sex relationship. She regarded her faith in Allah to be more crucial than religious rules.

Robin (thirty-seven years old, unmarried) identified as a *tomboi*. For most of her life, she rejected all forms of femininity imposed on her. She refused to wear a dress uniform during primary school until her school gave in and allowed her to wear pants. She refused to wear women's clothing, including female undergarments. She admired her girlfriend's cooking because women know how to cook; she joked that her cooking gave people diarrhea, even though she cooked for her employer every day.

When I asked about her views on the perceived conflict between Islam and lesbianism, she said:

> I have confessed to Allah about my mannish appearance and sexual preference. Allah listens to me. In short, I'm a good person, and Allah knows it.

Robin did not explain further what qualities a good person should possess. But she mentioned that some Muslims are not good even when they wear a *jilbab*:

> Some Muslims in *jilbab* came to me and told me that I'm wrong. They said, "You dress like a man. Allah doesn't accept women who dress in men's clothing." I said to them, "You're in a *jilbab*. It's very wrong for you to talk to people that way." Then, they went away.

Robin's Facebook page had a picture of her with a man inside a mosque; both were wearing men's white Islamic clothing. In the interview, Robin told me that she sometimes went to the Kowloon Mosque to listen to lectures conducted by Islamic teachers (*ustadz*). There are separate entrances for men and women at the mosque. Robin wore men's Islamic clothing and used the men's entrance. She was once stopped by a man at the entrance. However, Robin fought back and demanded to know why she was not allowed to enter the mosque. She then checked with another man, an Indonesian. The Indonesian man spoke for her and asked the guard to let her in. Robin eventually entered the mosque through the men's entrance.

Robin woke up at five in the morning to pray salat every day. When praying in her employer's home, she wore women's clothing to cover her hair, neck, arms, and legs. In the past, she wore men's when praying:

> From 2003 to 2007, I wore men's Islamic clothing. I even wore men's clothing when praying. But later I found it problematic. I was born a woman, so my

arms and legs must not be shown when praying. So, I changed to women's clothing when I pray. Other than praying, I usually wear men's clothing.

Robin's story is intriguing, as it shows how she addressed the conflict caused by her gender and sexual preference by positioning herself as a good person. I noted some of her good qualities. For instance, she persisted in waking up at five to pray every day, she was loyal to her girlfriend, and she was diligent and had established a good relationship with her employer. By sharing the confrontation with the Muslims in *jilbab*, she emphasized that wearing a *jilbab* does not mean that the person has good qualities.

Robin's choice of men's or women's Islamic clothing demonstrates how she negotiated her gender appearance in different spaces—the mosque (public space) or her employer's home (private space)—without compromising her religious piety. She referred to the rule of covering up for women when she prayed in a private setting. However, when she went to the mosque for lectures, she wore men's clothing. She did not let anyone see her feminine appearance.

Living in a Shelter with Islamic Traditions

The social position of an Indonesian migrant worker can be further complicated when she files a legal claim against her employer. In Hong Kong, labor law permits any migrant domestic worker to file a legal claim against her employer if the employer violates the employment contract or abuses the worker. However, the worker is not allowed to find a new employer in Hong Kong while the claim is pending because the conditions of employment state that migrant domestic workers can work for only the employer specified in the contract and on their visa (Home Affairs Bureau 2005), rendering them ultimately homeless. Fortunately, there are shelters in Hong Kong operated by charitable organizations that take in homeless migrant workers. Nini (twenty-three years old, unmarried) was one of the unlucky ones. Nini was assigned to stay at one of these shelters, which was operated by an Islamic organization. Her story below will show how Islamic organizations in Hong Kong attempt to correct the lesbian behavior of Indonesian women. Subjected to the position of a recipient, how did Nini respond to the Islamic expectations imposed on her?

I have known Nini since I started my field research in 2010. In 2011, she had a labor dispute with her employer, who asked Nini to work at two homes and never provided enough food for her. Nini filed a legal claim against her employer. While her case was pending, she stayed at the shelter. Given that the shelters operated by charitable organizations have very limited resources, there is always a shortage of beds. As the number of occupants already exceeded capacity, Nini was assigned to stay at another shelter run by an Islamic organization. Nini was a *tomboi* at the time.[2] Nini told me about her unpleasant experiences at the new shelter:

> The shelter is run by an Islamic organization. The Islamic teachers come and give lessons to us. They always tell me not to be with a woman and should be with a man. They know that I'm a lesbian. Every time they said this to me, I just kept smiling, but my heart totally disagreed with them. Every time I enter or leave the shelter, I cover up my hair, neck, arms, and legs as required by the shelter.

I was confused because Nini was wearing a short-sleeve crew-neck tee and a pair of short baggy pants; her lower legs were uncovered. I pointed at her exposed arms and legs when she mentioned the rule of covering up. Nini then showed me how she covered up when entering and leaving the shelter. She took out a pair of long-sleeve gloves, which covered her arms, and a light piece of fabric for covering her hair and neck. She also rolled down her pants to cover her lower legs. She said that the shelter did not require a full set of Islamic clothing but required women to cover their body when going out. Nini said she removed the gloves and headscarf once she left the shelter. She was annoyed with the clothing requirement, especially when it was so hot in the summer.

I was not surprised by Nini's revelations. I had never heard her speak about her religion or conflicting feelings caused by her same-sex relationship. But why did she stay in the Islamic-run shelter? Nini said that she did not select the shelter; the shelter chose her. According to Nini, the shelter targeted lesbian-like or *tomboi*-like women, so that they could correct their "wrong" and "sinful" behavior during their stay. Nini said that she was selected because of her *tomboi* appearance.

A week later, I visited Nini's shelter after she obtained approval from the housemother (*ibu asrama*). On the morning of the visit, Nini met up with me at the Wan Chai train station. When we were walking to the shelter, Nini told me that the housemother asked her several questions before granting permission. All were related to the gender and sexual reputation of the visitor. The first question was whether the visitor was a man or a woman. After she found out that the visitor was a woman, she proceeded to ask whether she was a *tomboi*. Nini told her that I was a *tomboi* (although she never directly confirmed this with me). The housemother then asked whether the *tomboi* was a *nakal* (naughty) one, who would flirt with other women or make sexual advances. Nini reassured her that I was a good person and would be well behaved. The housemother subsequently granted permission to Nini.

Nini and I arrived at the shelter, a two-bedroom apartment nestled in a fifteen-story building. The shelter was sparsely furnished and very clean and tidy.

---

2. Nini shifted between the two genders, *tomboi* and *cewek*. I have discussed her gender shifting practice in Chapter 2.

Nini introduced me to her three roommates, who were in one of the bedrooms. Nini had probably briefed them about my visit, so they were not surprised at my presence. Nini then led me to the living room to sit down. She pointed at an A4-size notice on the wall and read the text out loud in a low voice: "Tomboi dan lesbi di larang tinggal di sini."[3] The notice also provided an English version: "Tomboys and lesbians are banned from here." Nini recalled the day she first arrived and saw this notice. She felt that the notice was meant for her; therefore, she asked the housemother whether she could stay at the shelter. It was affirmed that Nini could stay at the shelter, but this did not mean that the shelter accepted Nini's behavior. In fact, the Islamic teachers constantly reminded Nini that it was wrong to have a same-sex relationship. There was another A4-size notice, which had a long list of rules and regulations on the general use of the shelter, such as keeping the area tidy and clean.

Nini's Muslim identity secured her a space in an Islamic-operated shelter. Her Muslim identity became salient in the process of receiving assistance from the shelters. I asked Nini how she felt about staying there. Nini said that she preferred the previous shelter because it was more liberal. Nini did not agree with the beliefs of the Islamic teachers and found the rules annoying. Despite the rules and regulations, she appreciated the shelter for offering her space and food. Therefore, she still respected the teachers and followed the rules.

Nini's story also demonstrates how Islamic organizations spread and reinforce their beliefs about gender and sexuality with the migrant domestic workers in Hong Kong through the shelters that they establish and operate. In this case, both the posted notice on the ban of *tomboi* and lesbians and the lectures given by the Islamic teachers subjected Nini to the position of a deviant Muslim in need of discipline.

Summary: Undoing and Doing Religion

The Muslim identity of the Indonesian women in this study was being undone in various situations. The Indonesian government, employment agents, and the women's parents attempted to downplay Muslim identity when they discovered that the Islamic principles are incompatible with the professional duties of domestic workers for Chinese families. The Indonesian government simply ignored the issue, the training centers improvised and taught the Indonesian women how to handle pork for their future Chinese employers, and the parents comforted their daughter and justified the violation of religious rules as part of their duties. The break from religious rules enabled the Indonesian women to produce the notion of *cuma di sini*, which emphasizes that they break the rules

---

3. In the Indonesian society, the term *tomboi* refers to a girl who has a boyish appearance without any implication of same-sex behavior. The notice emphasizes that both gender deviant (*tomboi*) and sexual deviant (*lesbi*) women are not allowed at the shelter.

only in Hong Kong. The Indonesian women in this study further extended the notion to justify their same-sex relationships in Hong Kong. Their narratives demonstrate that these women were aware of the conflict between Islam and their same-sex relationships, and so they avoided salat or wearing a *jilbab*. Seeing themselves as unclean, they maintained a distance from the sacred. They still highly respected their religion.

The Muslim identity of these Indonesian women was not wholly undone; instead, Muslim identity was marked and became salient in a number of special occasions. Champion's members said a short prayer together before a competition or in a birthday party. The more religious members served as prayer leaders. Nini's experience at the Islamic-operated shelter shows how her Muslim identity was marked and helped her gain a space at the shelter. Her story also shows how she negotiated her existence when she was in and out of the shelter, where the power relationship between the shelter and its occupants has never been equal.

A few of the Indonesian women in this study used their Islamic faith to reconcile the conflicting feelings caused by their same-sex relationships. Both Yanis and Robin emphasized that their faith was more crucial than the rules. Yanis prayed salat but not on a regular basis, and Robin wore men's Islamic clothing to the mosque. Their faith in Islam did not stop them from having a same-sex relationship but instead led them to confess their same-sex relationships to Allah and beg for forgiveness. The ethnographic account of the different ways of observing Islam has broadened and enriched the notion of piety among Indonesian workers in Hong Kong—they might not consider themselves as proper Muslims, but they have improvised ways to observe Islam, as they still regarded being Muslim as an integral part of themselves.

Alternative Gendered Expectations at the Employer's Home

Previous studies on migrant domestic workers depicted the home of the employer as a place of racial and class oppression (Yeoh and Huang 2010; Constable 1997; Ehrenreich and Hochschild 2002). Nicole Constable delineated how female Hong Kong employers (i.e., the wives) control the gender appearance of migrant domestic workers by establishing household rules; for example, no tight clothing, dresses, or makeup are to be worn at home. Through these household rules, the wives position migrant domestic workers as sexual threats (Constable 1997). The wives may prefer a masculine-looking domestic worker over a feminine one.

The *tomboi* in this study did not mention any difficulty in finding an employer. The following story about Jeni (twenty-eight, *tomboi*, unmarried) shows how her menswear and crew-cut hairstyle became an advantage at a job interview. When I first met Jeni, she wore her hair short, at around five inches in length. After a year, I heard from an Indonesian woman that Jeni had a lot of free time, as she had just finished a contract and was seeking a new employer. Therefore, I invited Jeni to meet me for an interview for this research project. On the day of the interview, I was surprised to see Jeni in a crew cut. Her hair was less than one inch in length. I asked her, "Your hair is really short now. Will there be any problem in finding yourself a new employer?" Jeni then shared with me the following story:

> My agent asked me why I cut my hair so short. I told her that there wasn't any reason. I just said it's simple and easy to manage. My new employer doesn't care what my hair looks like. When I was at the job interview, the wife asked me, "Do you wear revealing clothes?" I said, "Just what I'm wearing now. I like sportswear." She continued, "Do you wear nail polish?" I said, "Look at my fingers [no polish]." She asked, "Do you like children?" I told her I like kids a lot. Then, she said she wants to sign a contract with me.

During the job interview, the wife wanted to determine whether Jeni would be a sexual threat; therefore, she asked questions about Jeni's gender appearance. In response, Jeni was compelled to highlight her masculine appearance—sportswear and no nail polish. Her masculine qualities were advantageous to her in the workplace, as they fit the wife's gendered expectations.

Jeni's story was a win-win situation. She liked short hair; her employer liked it too. However, there are circumstances in which the worker is forced by her employer to cut off her hair. One of the Filipino domestic workers Constable (1997) interviewed was forced by her employer to crop off her shoulder-length hair into a man's style on the day she arrived at the employer's place. My investigation was inspired by this involuntary haircut—how does a worker think about herself and her sexuality after a significant change in gender appearance? I ask this question because the Indonesian women in my study were not isolated from the migrant community and the pop dance groups. A man's haircut could mean something desirable or be the mark of becoming a *tomboi* in their community.

Joy (thirty-nine, *tomboi*, married) had been working in Hong Kong for seven years. As a senior member in Champion, she helped with makeup and braided the hair of the *cewek* members taking part in fashion shows. She was so skilled at styling women's hair that she used wet tissue paper to wrap the hair before braiding to create waves after the hairbands and tissue papers were removed. I was amazed by her improvisation since the fashion shows took place at Victoria Park, which did not offer salon equipment. I was also amazed by her talent because I could not understand how a *tomboi* would acquire the knowledge and skills to carry out these tasks.

One Sunday, I met up with Joy and her friends at Victoria Park. We chatted about style and appearance, and Joy began to talk about herself. Her story explained why she, as a *tomboi*, knew how to style women's hair:

> In the past, I had long hair and was feminine. I wore dresses and high heels. When I began to work for my current employer seven years ago, the wife always complained that my hair was all over the floor. I was very sure that

the hair was not mine. It was hers. After several more complaints, I understood what she really meant—she wanted me to cut my hair short. I knew that she was jealous of me, so I changed my entire appearance. I cut my hair short and wore men's tees and shorts at home. I'm also glad that I changed because the wife went to China for a short period of time. It was only the husband, the kid, and me at home. The husband didn't touch me. I guess because I look like a man.

After her significant change in gender appearance, her *tomboi* friends began to comment about her:

Many of my friends in Hong Kong are *tomboi*. They told me that I have the wrong clothes. Mine are not as smart as the ones worn by *tomboi*. I followed their suggestions for clothing style and cut my hair even shorter. . . . In the following year, I met Alexis. After six months, I didn't know why but I had a crush on her. Then, I asked her whether she wanted to be my wife in Hong Kong. A week later, she said okay.

Joy's employer saw the feminine Joy as a sexual threat. The interaction between Joy and her employer subjected Joy to an inferior position: a foreign, lower-class woman whose sexual morality was questionable. Joy wanted to please her employer; therefore, she cut her hair short and wore men's tees. Her mannish appearance also produced a feeling of empowerment when she was left alone with the husband of her employer. Joy convinced herself that the husband did not harbor any sexual feelings for her because she looked like a man. She believed that her *tomboi* gender expression had become a form of protection for her.

Joy was not a docile body. She learned new meanings of her mannish appearance from her *tomboi* friends. Joy began to identify herself as a *tomboi*, as she could relate her bodily image with those of her *tomboi* friends. Joy was persuaded by her friends to dress in the fashion of a *tomboi* and become an intelligible person—a *tomboi* in *tomboi* fashion. Joy's *tomboi* identity was formed when her bodily image was considered to align with those of other *tomboi*. Her *tomboi* identity was affirmed when she established a relationship with a *cewek*.

Limiting Gender Ambiguity

In his study of black queer people in Detroit, Bailey noted their survival strategy. When black queer people went out during the day, they adjusted their gender appearance in accordance with the dominant gendered expectations; for example, male-bodied queer people avoided wearing tight pants to pass as ordinary men. They performed "double labor": (1) the work of material survival in a very homophobic public space and (2) the work of self-presentation of their queer identity (Bailey 2011, 374). The former supports the heteronormative gendered expectations in the larger society, while the latter expresses the queer self-identification of individuals.

Bailey's notion of double labor sheds light on the lived experiences of queer people who are racially marginalized. I use his notion to analyze how the *tomboi* manage the work of material survival in their employer's home. In the previous section, I discussed why the wives encouraged their migrant domestic worker to dress like a man. However, this does not mean that the wives were accepting of lesbians; rather, they could be homophobic. They neither wanted the worker to seduce their husband nor the worker to be a lesbian.

Hong Kong employers believe that they have the authority to comment on and control the gender appearance of their migrant domestic workers. Many *tomboi* are asked by their employers about their hairstyle. The most commonly asked question is, why do you cut your hair short like a man? The *tomboi* have developed a survival strategy of responding that short hair is easy to manage and convenient for work purposes. According to the *tomboi*, employers seldom continued to pursue them with more questions if the answer was for the benefit of the employers. By framing the answer in this way, the *tomboi* usually deflected further questions that might involve their sexuality.

Arief (twenty-five, *tomboi*, unmarried) worked for an employer who was strongly opposed to lesbianism. Arief said that her employer (a middle-aged couple with two children, twelve and fifteen years old) did not like her *tomboi* appearance and wanted her to dress in women's clothing. Her employer worked in a garment company and had access to clothing samples. Sometimes, her employer gave her samples of women's clothing as gifts. However, Arief refused to wear them. In response, her employer brought up the issue of sexuality and said to her, "We don't allow lesbians. It's gross." Arief wanted to protect her job, so she told her employer, "I don't like women. I'm not crazy." After hearing Arief's declaration, her employer felt relieved and finally accepted her masculine appearance. Her employer also renewed her contract. Arief secured her employment by denouncing lesbianism. Arief still received clothing samples, but they were men's clothing. Arief liked the clothes and wore them.

Associating gender presentation with work responsibilities is feasible only in the case of short hair. Complications arise when the focus is on the *tomboi*'s underwear. Hong Kong families wash their laundry in washing machines but do not use dryers. The common practice is to hang up clothes to dry in the apartment, in full view of every family member. When a *tomboi* hangs her men's underwear out to dry, it becomes evidence of her "perverse" sexuality.

Andra (twenty-six, *tomboi*, married) was employed by a seventy-year-old woman who lived alone. Her employer found that Andra never hung her bra to dry.

> When I was hanging out my clothes to dry, she came over to me and asked, "Don't you wear a bra?" I told her I don't wear a bra. Then, her daughter,

who came to visit her sometimes, asked me, "Why don't you wear a bra?" Grandma [her employer] then said to her daughter, "She [Andra] doesn't wear a bra at all. She's like a man."

Andra did not mention her employer taking any further action. Situated in an asymmetrical power relationship, Andra did not offer any rebuttal of her employer's comment.

Robin (thirty-seven, *tomboi*, unmarried) rejected femininity on both her upper and lower body. For her upper body, she did not wear a bra. She said her breasts are very flat; I could not see their shape, as she always wore loose-fitting clothes. For her lower body, she did not wear women's underpants but men's. She said that all her employers, both previous and current, found out that she wore men's underpants when she hung her underpants to dry:

> My current employer, a grandpa and his son and daughter-in-law, see me hanging my clothes out to dry. They know that I wear men's underpants and I don't wear a bra.

Robin was very confident in her abilities, as she had been working in Hong Kong for more than fifteen years. She knew that her employers were satisfied with her skills. For example, a friend of Robin's employer had stains on her clothing, and her migrant domestic worker did not know how to remove them. The woman called Robin's employer for advice. Robin's employer did not know, so she asked Robin. Robin suggested that she could remove the stains, and if the friend brought the offending piece of clothing to her, Robin would fix the problem. Without disappointing anyone, Robin removed all the stains. Later, when the woman came to pick up her garment, she complimented Robin in front of the employer. Robin was therefore fully aware of her exceptional work performance. She did not believe that any of her employers would fire her just because of her appearance or male underwear. Therefore, she continued to hang it out to dry.

I did not survey every *tomboi* about her choice of underwear. The stories about underwear were initiated by Andra and Robin during their interview. My point in discussing the hanging of underwear out to dry is to highlight the vulnerability of *tomboi* in the home of their employer. By vulnerability, I mean the inability of the *tomboi* to control how their employers perceive their gender and sexuality. The act of hanging out their underwear (i.e., no bra, men's underpants) subjects them to a perverted position. Their preference of undergarments is revealed and seriously contradicts the employer's belief about a "normal" woman.

While Hong Kong employers seem to tolerate, accept, or even encourage the gender ambiguity of their Indonesian domestic workers, that is, having short hair and wearing young men's clothing, there is also a *limit* to the gender ambiguity accepted in the home of the employers. *Tomboi* need to clarify to their employers that they are not lesbians; they should wear women's undergarments to designate their female body. Those who venture beyond the tolerated limit are confronted by their employer.

When Workers Become Customers ...

How does the relationship between Hong Kong people and the Indonesian women change when the latter are not in the role of workers during their days off? When they go shopping and eat out, their role changes from worker to customer. As noted by Pei-cha Lan (2006), migrant workers commonly experience mistreatment based on class and race even on their days off. In her study of Indonesian domestic workers in Taiwan, Indonesian women felt discriminated against by the sales staff in the major department stores. In fact, most of the Indonesian women in Lan's study had never visited upscale department stores. They usually shopped in the underground Metro Mall or hung out in karaoke boxes operated by Indonesian Chinese. Their Hong Kong counterparts have a similar experience. The Indonesian women in my study seldom frequented upscale stores or venues, which they regarded to be the domain of Hong Kong people. Instead, they preferred to frequent venues that mainly served Indonesians, for instance, private karaoke rooms.

Nevertheless, even in venues that mainly cater to the Indonesian domestic workers, race and class identities still matter. Instead of respecting the Indonesian women as customers, I found that the business owners scrutinized them and controlled the space by limiting who could enter the venue. In the following, I examine the types of control and rules that were imposed in two types of venues: (1) private karaoke rooms and (2) monthly rental rooms. I visited both types of venues with these Indonesian women and observed how they were treated by the business owners, who are Hong Kong people.

The first event was a birthday celebration for Michelle, the mother of Champion. I was invited to her birthday party, which was held in a private karaoke room. I followed the Champion members and arrived on the sixth floor of an old fifteen-story commercial building in Causeway Bay. The karaoke room was located inside an office suite. Unlike licensed karaoke bars, this kind of karaoke room is illegal. Therefore, no signs were posted to indicate that it was a karaoke business. I followed the members into the office suite. A man and a woman, Hong Kong people in their early forties, immediately stood up and said, "Men can't come here!" They were sitting close to the door and could clearly see who was coming and going. I knew then that they had mistaken me for a man. Michelle explained to them in Cantonese that I am a woman. The man was a bit embarrassed and said to his colleague, "I told you she's not a man!" Then, they let us into the karaoke room. The room was about 150 square feet in size. Apart from the karaoke equipment, there was an old couch and a folding table. Some of the early guests had already started to sing and dance in a small group. The

Hong Kong man and woman did not come inside the room again until the party was finished.

A few months later, I went with the Champion members to another private karaoke room. This one was also hidden in a commercial building in Causeway Bay, just a few blocks from the previous one. There was a sign that said "Sunshine Internet Services" on the main door. The business was primarily an internet café, with a hidden karaoke business in the private rooms of the office suite. An A4-size notice was posted on the wall next to the main door that said in capital letters, "warning!!! not allow men chat here!" "perhatian!!!dilarang keras pria masuk di sini." The notice in both English and Indonesian was issued by the Sunshine Company, with its business seal stamped on the notice. When I entered the internet café, there was no receptionist or security guard. I walked to one of the rooms, and nobody scrutinized my gender.

Rental rooms in Hong Kong are another venue to investigate how Hong Kong landlords scrutinize their tenants. Eva (thirty years old), who was not in any of the pop dance groups, spent most of her holidays in a rental room in Yuen Long. I knew Eva because she was employed by my classmate's parents. My classmate said that Eva was attracted to women and could be a potential informant for my research project. She introduced Eva to me when I went to visit her on a weekday afternoon. Eva was very friendly with me. After listening to my research purpose, she said that she could talk to me. She gave me her mobile phone number for further contact. After a few days, I called Eva and asked to meet with her on a Sunday. She then invited me to visit her rental room, which she considered to be her real home in Hong Kong.

The rental room was in a remote village, a thirty-minute walk from the Yuen Long West Rail Station. I followed Eva and arrived at a single-story building. There were about ten rental rooms, two shared bathrooms, and one kitchen. Eva rented one of the rooms. Eva and I walked by her Indonesian neighbors, who were eating breakfast in their room with their door open. They invited us to join them for breakfast, but we turned them down and went to Eva's room. Her room was around eighty square feet. In this tiny space, there were a TV set, hi-fi speakers, sleeping mats, two rice cookers, and some basic utensils. Eva invited me to sit on her sleeping mat. She did not close the door. Anyone who walked by could clearly see in the room. It appeared to be a type of courtesy to keep the door open. Her neighbors were Indonesian domestic workers. The room opposite was occupied by two Indonesian women. One looked like a *tomboi*, and the other one was feminine-looking with long hair. The place became lively and vibrant as the morning went by. Most of the tenants arrived. Some started to cook meals while others enjoyed loud music in their rooms.

Eva said that she had rented the room for more than a year at a monthly rate of HKD 800 (USD 103). She had been working in Hong Kong for seven years. In the past six years, she went to Victoria Park or shopping malls on her holidays.

After renting the room, she would go every Sunday in the morning and stay until 7 p.m. The law in Hong Kong stipulates that Eva cannot live in any place other than her employer's home. Eva still considers it is worth renting the room even if she cannot stay overnight. Afterward, we chatted for a while until her lover, Annie, arrived and joined us. Unlike the other couples that I met in the Champion dance group, Eva and Annie did not show their affection by holding hands or hugging each other. Although I saw their picture in a photo frame engraved "I Love You," I was still unable to confirm that they were lovers until I asked them directly in an interview on another day.

The female landlord came in the afternoon, accompanied by two other women. They were Hong Kong people, around fifty years old. Eva said one of the women was the landlord's sister. They came to collect the rent. One of the women stopped by Eva's room and stared at me. She asked, "Are you a woman?" Her question alerted the female landlord, who then came over to assess the situation. I told them that I was a woman. Nevertheless, the woman continued, "Why don't you dress like a woman?" Before I could say anything, the female landlord said to her, "She just doesn't like to dress like a woman." Eva said to the landlord, "I wouldn't bring any men here." The female landlord and the woman were satisfied with Eva's affirmation, left us alone, and then sat somewhere else to chat. Eva told me that the landlord did not allow tenants to have men over.

The female landlord did not leave immediately after collecting the rental money. She walked around as if she was supervising her Indonesian tenants. When Eva was frying bean curds in the kitchen, the landlord approached her and asked Eva to open the window for ventilation. In fact, Eva had already done so, which she explained to the landlord. However, the landlord was not satisfied and opened the window much wider. When she saw a space cooler in Eva's room, she said to Eva, "That's a waste of money! Having a fan is already enough." It was obvious that a space cooler would consume more electricity, and the landlord was responsible for paying the utility fees.

Indonesian women were scrutinized in the karaoke rooms and rental rooms. They were prohibited by the business owner or their landlord from inviting male guests onto the premises, even though as customers they should have the right to do so. Eva's rental room was not a shared room; therefore, the rule prohibiting men from visiting was not justified. These irrational rules clearly show the intersectionality of class, race, and sexuality—the women's class background and racial identity was reduced to "maids coming from a poor country"; their morality and sexuality were questioned by the business owner and the landlord, who assumed that these "foreign maids" were promiscuous and would readily engage in sex with men. The illogical rules reflected the underlying assumptions that subject Indonesian women to a very low status with the stigma of promiscuity.

Summary: Surviving in the City

Examining the experience of the Indonesian women and their treatment in their employer's home, private karaoke rooms, and rental rooms, I found that these Indonesian women were regarded by Hong Kong people as a threat to the city's sexual morality, regardless of the change in their role from domestic worker to customer on their days off. Hong Kong people, for the sake of protecting their domestic or business reputation, have developed notorious rules, both formal and informal, to control the gender appearance of these Indonesian women and question their sexual morality and sexual orientation. In the process of carrying out these rules, some effects are inadvertently produced. The rules induce and produce a space that allows Indonesian women to develop a *tomboi* identity and cultivate same-sex relationships.

I am not suggesting that Indonesian domestic workers become lesbians just because employers request short hair and discourage hyperfeminine clothing. Rather, I am saying that Indonesian domestic workers are active agents who make sense of and enjoy their new gender appearance by borrowing the meanings of masculine traits and the images of *tomboi* from the migrant community. It is noteworthy that employers have a limited tolerance for gender ambiguity. *Tomboi* are designated by their employer as female bodies and are expected to be "normal" women. Questions follow if Indonesian women are suspected to be lesbians or are found wearing men's underpants.

In the private karaoke rooms and the rental rooms, men are explicitly excluded. The practical reason behind this rule was not very important to these Indonesian women. To them, the impact of the rule was its insinuated moral message: it is bad (because it is a violation of the rule) to spend time with men; decent women should confine their social circle to only women. Same-sex relationships, on the contrary, are left unmarked and tolerated in these spaces. I was barred from entering a karaoke room because the business owners mistook me for a man. After my biological sex was clarified, they had no interest in my relationship with the Indonesians or whether I was a lesbian. In Eva's rental room, the female landlord was not concerned with the status of my relationship with Eva. She had no interest in learning in any of the intimate relationships taking place in the rental rooms, either between Eva and Annie or other *tomboi-cewek* couples. The space became inadvertently receptive to same-sex intimacy as it was left unmarked.

The notorious rules of Hong Kong employers, business owners, and landlords are originally assumed to be racially motivated. Subjected to a powerless position, Indonesian women are forced to follow these rules. However, they are never docile bodies. Instead, they are active agents who negotiate their existence by drawing meaning and support from the migrant community. They have developed strategies as well as the patience to handle questions from employers, karaoke room keepers, and landlords. A space can accept *tomboi* and same-sex intimacy, if they do not make the Hong Kong people acknowledge their same-sex relationship.

4
Imaginings of Home

The Hong Kong immigration ordinance stipulates that migrant domestic workers are allowed to legally reside in Hong Kong only based on employment. A worker must leave the territory of Hong Kong immediately if she fails to secure employment within two weeks of the completion of a contract. In addition, Indonesian ideology assumes that migrant workers will return home eventually because labor migration is only a temporary stint. The Indonesian women in this study therefore expected to return home permanently when they no longer wanted to work as migrant domestic workers.

These Indonesian women imagined their future home to be in Indonesia, not Hong Kong. In this chapter, the focus of investigation will be on these Indonesian women's imagined home. Home has been imperative for understanding the power dynamics and negotiations between heteronormative family expectations and the desires of female or queer subjects in feminist and LGBT studies (see Fortier 2001; Mohanty and Martin 2003). By examining the imagined home of the migrant women, I unravel how Indonesian women reconciled their future and their desires with family expectations. Did they imagine a new home with their same-sex lover? Did they think that it was even possible to have a home with their same-sex lover in Indonesia? As Arjun Appadurai said, imagination is no longer mere fantasy or simple escape but has become "an organized field of social practices" and a form of negotiation between individuals and the fields of possibility (2002, 49). These women's imaginings of home matter because imagination can direct people to create new meanings in life.

I suggest taking a transnational perspective to examine the intertwining relationship between the present and the future; that is, the desires and practices of the Indonesian women that took place in Hong Kong and their imagined home in Indonesia. Situating Indonesian women in a transnational frame complicates the meaning of sexuality by taking into consideration gendered expectations, the cultural specificities of particular locales, and political economies of the family, as well as the refigurations of identities and imaginaries (Povinelli and Chauncey

1999; F. Y. Lai 2018b). A transnational frame also recognizes contacts and transactions of travel as part of the knowledge production that constitutes and creates new subjects (Grewal and Kaplan 2001). The contacts and knowledge that the Indonesian women had and made and obtained in Hong Kong enabled them to constitute imaginaries of their future life; these imaginaries informed and shaped the women's desires.

Previous studies have shown that there is a tendency among researchers to represent home as a universal patriarchy—a heteronormative locale in which female and queer subjects are oppressed or which they are forced to leave in order to achieve liberation (Gopinath 2005; Manalansan 2002; Mohanty and Martin 2003). The problem with this representation is its disregard for the cultural specificities of particular locales as well as the imaginaries created by female and queer subjects in a migratory context. I find that "remaking the space of home from within" by Gayatri Gopinath (2005, 14) to be very useful in the analysis of the imagined home of these migrant women. Gopinath argued that queer people might stay in an oppressive home and at the same time denounce heteronormative logic, as shown in her analysis of *Fire*, a film by Deepa Mehta, in which two sisters-in-law become lovers (14–15). Thus, as Gopinath puts it, home should not be considered a place that has been left behind by queer people but as a space they remake by cultivating homoerotic relationships there.

Sexuality cannot be viewed as a simple binary of "normative heterosexuality versus nonnormative homosexuality." Asian queer subjectivities are complex and cannot be confined to this simple binary, as they constantly negotiate family responsibilities and are expected to maintain close ties with their parents. In Indonesia, it is very common for parents to pressure their single adult daughters to marry. While I look at the movement and agency of these migrant women, I also heed the boundaries that cannot be crossed because of cultural constraints (Grewal and Kaplan 2001). I examine how these Indonesian women improvised ways to negotiate with their families in the process of imagining their future and how heteronormative expectations and their same-sex desires were intertwined in their imaginings of home.

This chapter examines the sexual subjectivity of these Indonesian women by studying their projected imaginings of home. Situated in a migratory context, how did their contacts and transactions of travel enable them to imagine a future home with their same-sex lover? How did these imaginaries transform the space of home by *queering* the space, that is, by subverting the heteronormative logic of home? How did those who decided to refrain from crossing the boundaries of heteronormativity after returning to Indonesia fulfill their same-sex desires and make sense of their same-sex practices in Hong Kong?

Home and Heteronormativity

In Indonesia, the concept of home is highly connected to marital status. Young unmarried adults, both men and women, reside with their parents (Nobles and Buttenheim 2008). Therefore, the home of unmarried women is that of their parents. Women who are in their early twenties are expected to marry and form a separate household with their husband and children (Naafs 2013). The home of married women is the household that they share with their husband and children (Nilan 2008).

Although women's living arrangements (i.e., location and cohabitants) are tightly regulated, some are able to negotiate these expectations and live with their female partner as long as the couple remains silent about their same-sex relationship and does not demand formal or public recognition of any kind. Saskia Wieringa studied a female same-sex community in Jakarta (the capital of Indonesia), which comprised several hundred lower-class women, who were mostly first-generation immigrants from other islands. The couples lived together, and their living arrangements were accepted by their neighbors. The neighbors called the masculine partners "uncle"; the feminine partners were regarded as normal women and participated in the women's neighborhood activities. Several of the couples mutually cared for children from earlier marriages. Although neighbors may well have understood that these living arrangements were unusual, there was no condemnation as long as the couples did not speak out about their same-sex relationships. Wieringa (2007) showed that different definitions and levels of normality were at play in Indonesian society.

Urbanization and the increasing participation of women in economic life through work contribute to the formation of female same-sex communities. In part, this is because labor migration to cities like Jakarta provides a valid reason for women to live outside the parental home (Wieringa 2007). However, it remains unlikely that same-sex desiring women living in the parental home will establish a separate household with a same-sex partner. In her study on female same-sex relationships in Padang, a metropolitan area in Sumatra, Blackwood (2010) found that only two couples, out of her twenty-two informants, lived together. Although the couples were cohabiting, other kin members were also living with them. The couples concealed their relationship and refrained from any intimate behavior in front of their kin. The couples were not suspected to be lesbians because of the prevalent homosocial activities in the larger Southeast Asian context, where two women sharing a bed is generally associated with sisterhood (Blackwood 2010; Sinnott 2004). The concept of home is heteronormatively structured around the social tradition of marriage and childbearing; this is naturalized to the extent that same-sex relationships may go undetected.

Emotions about Home

Before examining the imaginings of home projected by the Indonesian women in this study, it is important to understand their views of their actual home in Indonesia. In the process of labor migration and experiencing same-sex relationships in Hong Kong, their feelings toward home in Indonesia might have changed. These changed emotions and views are important to analyze here because they influence decisions on whether the women will return to their original heteronormative home or establish a separate household, and hence a new home, with their female partner.

In this respect, these Indonesian women were concerned about their relationship with their (1) parents, (2) community (i.e., relatives and neighbors), and (3) husband and children when they voiced their feelings about home in Indonesia. I discuss each of these concerns in the following.

(1) Relationship with parents

These Indonesian women believed that their parents would not accept and would be very angry about their same-sex relationship. A common view was that a same-sex partner would become a source of dispute with their parents. Since the Indonesian women highly valued their relationships with their parents, it made more sense to conceal this part of their life than to risk upsetting their parents or worse.

Even though these women did not disclose their same-sex relationship to their parents, their parents reprimanded them based on rumors or suspicions that they were in a same-sex relationship. Two Indonesian women said that their former girlfriend retaliated against them by calling their parents in Indonesia. Michelle (thirty-two, *cewek*, unmarried) recalled:

> My ex was awful! She called my parents and told them that I am a lesbian. That's why my parents know [that I am a lesbian]. Now whenever I call my parents, they check on me and ask, "Are you still a lesbian?" I just lie and tell them that I am looking for guys.

Michelle lied to her parents because she valued her relationship with them highly and did not want to upset them any more.

Similarly, the parents of another Indonesian woman became suspicious when she showed them pictures that featured a *tomboi*. A confrontation ensued, and her parents asked whether she was in love with a *tomboi* in Hong Kong. She immediately denied it, although she had had a *tomboi* partner in Hong Kong for almost two years. These examples illustrate a common strategic practice vis-à-vis parents and the importance of maintaining good relationships with them.

(2) Relationships with the community

These Indonesian women held the common view that neighbors and relatives in their home village liked to gossip, particularly about their sexual morality. According to the Indonesian moral value system, women's bodies and sexuality belong not to them but to their families. According to Islamic beliefs, fathers are the moral guardian of their unmarried daughters (Bennett 2005). If they fail to control their daughters, parents are the objects of defamation. The ultimate effect of gossip is to put pressure on the parents to maintain the sexual purity of their unmarried daughters specifically and hence maintain family and social honor more generally.

Yanis (twenty-seven, *cewek*, married) shared her memory of home:

> In Indonesia, I feel like I can't do anything. It's so easy to get criticized for something or people talk behind your back. In Indonesia, you have to be on your best behavior. If you did something that doesn't seem quite right, people will point their finger at you. They'll talk about you. . . . I had several male friends when I was in high school. Sometimes, the boys came over to my place. But actually, boys and girls should not hang out together. My neighbors were saying behind my back, "That Yanis has men hanging out at her house every single day."

In recalling her experience as the object of defamation, Yanis also imagined that she would have to be on her best behavior after returning to Indonesia. Although Yanis's memory of home was directly related not to same-sex relationships but to normative expectations of women in general, she already considered her same-sex relationship to be a violation of the heteronormative expectations of the community. She did not think that the relationship would ever meet the approval of those in her village.

Samuel (thirty, *tomboi*, unmarried) maintained a close relationship with her mother and would call home on a regular basis. When her same-sex relationship in Hong Kong was becoming more mature, Samuel disclosed the relationship to her mother over the phone because she really wanted her mother to know about this important part of her life. Although her parents had already accepted her same-sex sexuality, Samuel imagined that the people in her home village would not be receptive to her same-sex relationship. Samuel was the only woman in this study whose parents accepted her same-sex relationship:

> In Indonesia, living with my parents . . . well [Samuel sighs], I will be fine, but the community would not like it. They wouldn't accept it. Anyway, Ahan [Samuel's girlfriend] and I are moving somewhere farther from our families.

In her memory of home, there were no lesbians in the village. There were no role models for Samuel to imagine how she would maintain a same-sex relationship and live in her village. Samuel told me that one of her friends in Indonesia was also a lesbian. This friend was a university student and lived with her girlfriend in a boarding house. Having a lesbian friend back in Indonesia created the means for Samuel to imagine the possibility of maintaining a lesbian relationship in Indonesia, albeit one located far away from the family home.

(3) Relationship with husband and children

Among the Indonesian women in my study, twelve were married. I identified two major reasons for these women to leave their husband to work overseas. The first was that working overseas provided them with a legitimate opportunity to leave their husband in Indonesia. Two of the women said that they had been physically abused by their husband. Another two indicated they were pressured by their family to marry their husband, even though they did not love him. These four women knew that working overseas would be a feasible way for them to leave their husband and at the same time support themselves. Therefore, they decided to work in Hong Kong.

The second reason was that working overseas provided them with a substantial income for improving their husband and children's quality of life in Indonesia. Not only would they pay for their family's daily expenses, but they also aimed to save money to buy a house in Indonesia. The women were at first very committed to this plan and regularly remitted money back to their husband. However, upon discovering that their husband had been involved in affairs, they stopped supporting him. Formally speaking, Indonesian marriage law permits a Muslim man to take a second wife, but this requires court approval and permission from the first wife (Rinaldo 2011). The marriage law shows that society generally prioritizes the ideal of monogamous marriage over the practice of polygamy. Therefore, the Indonesian women in this study were naturally upset about the affairs. Still, only one formally divorced her husband. The others explained that they had not returned to Indonesia since they found out about the affairs.

Among the married women, seven were mothers. Two said that their husband was responsible for taking care of their children while they were away. The other five said that their own parents were the caretakers of their children. Interestingly, their relationships with their children were very different between these two groups of mothers. The two mothers (Iman, thirty-two, *tomboi*, and Lestari, thirty-five, *cewek*) whose children were under the care of their husband said that they had very limited or even no contact with their children because their husband forbade any phone contact. The men had already established new households with other women, and the children were under the care of these new households. Since the children had new "moms," the men did not want their first wife to call anymore. Lestari said that her husband changed his home phone number, and her ten-year-old son did not own a cellphone. Therefore, she had not been in touch with her son for a few years already. Iman was somewhat more fortunate in that her daughter was already in high school, and so she sent money directly to her daughter to buy a cellphone. Iman could therefore call and maintain contact with her daughter on a regular basis.

The second group (the other five mothers) consisted of women whose children were under the care of their own parents, and typically they enjoyed very close relationships with their children. They fulfilled the role of good mother by regularly calling their children and sending adequate money back home for their school fees and daily expenses. They also brought expensive gifts (e.g., laptops) from Hong Kong to Indonesia during their contract-end holidays. These transnational mothers provided both emotional and material support to their children. Moreover, these mothers also allowed their female partners to converse with their children over the phone, thereby establishing informal chosen kinship connections alongside the heteronormative ones. The children ranged from a few years old to twelve. The mothers introduced their female partner to their children as one of their close friends in Hong Kong, and so the children did not know about their mother's same-sex relationship. The female partners also showed their love and care for these children by conversing with them over the phone and sending gifts.

Imagining a New Home, Imagining Cities

Among the women who said that they wanted to live with their girlfriend after returning to Indonesia, all were involved in a stable relationship with their partner for more than a year in Hong Kong. The longest relationship was six years. When the couple shared their views of the future with me, both *tomboi* and *cewek* held the same view in that they wanted to maintain their same-sex relationship in Indonesia. The oldest couple was thirty-two and thirty-six years old, and the youngest couple was twenty and twenty-two years old. Half were unmarried. Gender (*tomboi* or *cewek*), age, or marital status was not a determining factor in deciding whether they wanted to live with their female lover in the future. What mattered was having a stable partner or a satisfying relationship at the time of the interview.

In their imaginings of home, their new homes would be somewhere outside of their old homes. They said that they would move away from their natal family or the home of their husband. Half said that they wanted to move to a large city in Indonesia, to live in Jakarta, Yogyakarta, or Kediri on the island of Java. Since most of the women in this study were from the island of Java (only two were not Javanese), they were inclined to live there after returning to Indonesia. Why would these women believe that a large city would be a suitable place to settle? What were they imagining about these cities? Where did their imagination of cities originate?

In their imagination of cities, these women did not mention anything related to LGBT scenes or queer spaces. Although Jakarta is the largest city in Indonesia and known for its nightclubs where lesbians meet each other (Murray 1999), none of the women in my study commented on the lesbian scene in Jakarta. When they talked about their future, they were concerned with earning an income. The women in this study were from the rural areas, and most did not have a post-secondary education. Therefore, if they were to move to the city to start a new life, this act may not necessarily signify liberation but repression because of their class and education background. As noted by Martin Manalansan (2003) in his study of Filipino gay migrants in New York, the men experience restructured inequalities caused by race and class through migration. The dominant model that views queer migration from rural/less-developed to urban/well-developed areas as a movement from repression to liberation neglects class differences and material survival (Luibhéid 2008). These Indonesian migrant women were aware of the disadvantages of living in the cities without cultural capital. While they recognized these disadvantages, they did not easily succumb but instead imagined ways of earning an income in the cities.

As noted by Grewal and Kaplan (2001), the contacts and transactions of travel are part of the knowledge production that constitutes and creates new subjects. I examined their travel and work experience in both Indonesia and Hong Kong. Some of these women had worked in Indonesian cities as restaurant servers, factory workers, and nannies. Therefore, it is important to ask, what knowledge is produced in the process of migration that enables these women to imagine ways of earning an income in the city?

Nini (twenty-three, *cewek*, unmarried) worked in a restaurant in Bali, owned by a relative, before she became a migrant domestic worker. She was only eighteen when she worked in Bali. During her six months of employment there, Nini did not earn one single dollar because her relative used her as free labor. Although Nini was not able to earn any money in Bali, she learned about operating a business. The work experience in Bali constituted a form of knowledge that enabled Nini to imagine and construct her future. Nini was a *tomboi* when she was in a relationship with Citra (twenty-six, *cewek*, married). Before they broke up, the couple shared their plans to move to Yogyakarta with me. Nini's home village is about a three-hour drive from there. Citra is from East Java, about an eleven-hour drive from there. Nini had been to Yogyakarta, but not Citra. The couple said that they wanted to open a food stall (*warung*). Nini shared her plans with me:

> We want to open a food stall. Citra cooks and I take orders from the customers. There are lots of tourists in Yogyakarta. This means a lot of people would eat out.

In her imagination of her new home with Citra, Nini integrated her work experience in Bali with her impression of Yogyakarta. She imagined that opening a food stall would generate money because there are many tourists, just like at her relative's restaurant in Bali. Her work experience in Bali opened a window for Nini to construct her future and imagine her new home with Citra in Indonesia.

As noted by Umut Erel, migrants are able to create new forms of knowledge and cultural capital in the process of migration. In her study of skilled women who migrated from Turkey to Germany, Erel (2010) demonstrated how a Turkish woman self-produces herself as a cultured person by establishing Turkish music choirs and Turkish theater groups in Germany. I apply Erel's findings to analyze how migrants (including low-skilled migrant workers) create cultural capital by using resources that became available to them in the process of migration. The following story of Iman will show how she gained cultural capital in Hong Kong, which allowed her to imagine her social mobility in Indonesia—she would operate her own business in the city.

Iman (thirty-two, *tomboi*, married) and Lestarti (thirty-five, *cewek*, married) planned to live in Kediri, a city of 250,000 people in East Java, after they returned from working in Hong Kong. Kediri is Iman's hometown, but the couple was not afraid of returning there. Iman said that her parents passed away many years ago. She informed her only older sister that she would buy a house and live with a female friend after returning to Kediri. She also told her sister that her husband had another woman and children, and so she would not return to his home. Her older sister did not challenge her plans. Therefore, Iman assumed that her sister had given her blessing.

The couple shared their plans of living in Kediri with me:

Lestari:	I want to work two more contracts, and then return to Indonesia. I want to have a house and live with Iman. She will work and I will stay at home.
Iman and Lestari:	We want to buy a house in Kediri because there are factories and hospitals there.
Lestari:	When we have enough money, we will buy one more house and rent it out.
Iman:	I want to improve my computer skills.
Lestari:	She wants to improve her computer skills so that she can make music files, photos, and videos for clients. There are lots of opportunities to do business in Kediri.

In the future home projected by Iman and Lestari, Kediri is a place full of business opportunities, not gossip. Although Iman was optimistic about the business opportunities in Kediri, she was aware that she lacked the skills to operate a business. In Hong Kong, Iman owned a laptop and a digital camera. She liked to upload her personal pictures onto Facebook from her laptop. Iman knew how to use a computer, but she did not think that her current skills were enough to establish a business. Therefore, she wanted to learn more computer skills to make videos for clients. She was aware of computer classes that target migrant domestic workers in Hong Kong. These classes are organized by nongovernmental organizations (NGOs) and are offered on Sundays at affordable prices, which was around USD 40 per month. Iman was aware that these resources offered by the NGOs would increase her cultural capital (that is, her computer skills), which would contribute to social mobility before returning to Indonesia.

Informed by their experiences and transactions in the process of migration, these Indonesian women imagined that they could make a living with their same-sex partner in the city. Their imaginings of home, in turn, constituted their sexual subjectivity. They believed that they could live with their same-sex lover in Indonesia, and they had the autonomy to choose their own path. Whether they eventually realized their imaginary home is not the focus of this study; what matters are the meanings produced by the imagined home and how the subjects acted when they placed such trust in their imaginaries.

Remaking the Space of Home

The Indonesian women in my study who imagined building a new home with their female partner in Indonesia seemed like proper lesbian subjects under the gay liberation discourse of declaring independence from family expectations. However, their sexual subjectivities were more complex and could not be encapsulated by the liberation model. None of these women planned to announce herself as a lesbian after returning to Indonesia. Although they would not be bothered by village gossip after moving to a big city, they still did not want to make their same-sex relationship public. They did not want to draw attention to their nonnormative relationships. In her study of lesbian couples in Jakarta, Saskia Wieringa noted that the couples did not force their neighbors to openly acknowledge their same-sex relationships. Although neighbors might already have understood (*mengerti*) that the two women were in a sexual union, they did not condemn the couple as long as their love was not brought to the public surface of knowing (*tahu*), which is associated with speaking. Wieringa argued that there is great emphasis on social harmony (*rukun*) in Indonesia. People avoid disclosing personal matters that might "rupture the tenuous and unstable religious and social consensus" (2007, 83).

In following Wieringa, I examine how the Indonesian women imagined their interactions with their new neighbors in the city and their relationships with family members in their natal homes. More than mental images, their imagination of home shaped their social practices (Appadurai 2002). What did these women do to fulfill their same-sex desire without publicly upsetting heteronormative expectations?

Sisterhood as camouflage

The imagined home of Iman (thirty-two, *tomboi*, married) drastically changed over the years that she had been working in Hong Kong. Her original imagined home was entirely destroyed, the one for which she worked so hard in Hong Kong and helped her husband obtain a good job in Indonesia. Separation from her husband was the catalyst for developing a serious same-sex relationship in Hong Kong and rebuilding her imagination of home. However, this time, the imagined space and the meaning of home were entirely new. Iman was not a wife anymore but a husband. The couple imagined that their new home might create suspicion or gossip from the neighbors because they were two adult women without a husband. They assumed that their neighbors might be curious and ask about their relationship. Therefore, they already thought of an explanation: "We'll just tell the neighbors that we are sisters." Even though their future neighbors might not be able to interfere or affect their material survival, that is, running a small business of video and digital production in Kediri, they were still concerned about gossip.

The couple also avoided the word "lesbian" or "lover" when they shared their plans with their natal families. Lestari (Iman's girlfriend) told her parents and siblings that she was not returning to her natal or her husband's home; instead, she was moving to Kediri with her friend. As noted by Wieringa (2007), there is great emphasis on social harmony in Indonesia. The couple intended to maintain social harmony. They did not consider speaking out about their same-sex relationship to their neighbors or family members to be a wise way to survive in Indonesia.

Their imagination of home shaped their practices in Hong Kong—they continued to work hard in Hong Kong for two more contracts, that is, four years, to save sufficient funds for a house and a small business in Kediri. The couple also redefined the meaning of home as homoerotic; it was no longer defined as a married heterosexual couple but as two women living together. While this same-sex couple followed the heteronormative ideal of "the husband (Iman) going to work and the wife (Lestari) staying at home," they transgressed the boundary between husband and wife—Iman, a former wife, became the husband in the imagined home. Their desire for this imagined home was filled with Iman's sense of masculinity and Lestari's sense of femininity.

Parenting a girlfriend's children

Bailey (2013) reminds us that the notion of home does not necessarily depend on the physical space of home. He argues that black queer people establish their sense of home through parent-children relationships with people who have no blood ties with each other. The labor of parenting, as conceived by Bailey, is useful for understanding how Indonesian women imagine home, especially the couples who had children with their former husband. The following discussion focuses on the home imagined by Grace (thirty-six, *tomboi*, widow), who was in a relationship with Sharon (thirty-two, *cewek*, divorced, mother of two children, who are six and twelve). I will show how Grace realized some parts of her imagined home by parenting Sharon's children. That is, Grace remade the space of home by fulfilling her desire for Sharon and her love for Sharon's two daughters.

Grace and Sharon had been in a relationship for more than six years in Hong Kong. Both were Christians. Grace was born in Manado, North Sulawesi, and Sharon was from Malang, Java. Grace married in her early twenties; however, her husband died after two years. In Indonesia, *janda* refers to women who lost their husband, by either death or divorce. *Janda* are labelled with a bundle of pejorative meanings concerning their presumed sexual availability to men and lack of economic resources (Mahy, Winarnita, and Herriman 2016; Wieringa 2012). Some *janda* in Petra Mahy's study used migration to avoid marginalization in their home village. This was the case for Grace. She first worked in Singapore and then in Hong Kong. Among the Indonesian women in this study, Grace was the only one who obtained a bachelor's degree. Despite her academic qualifications, she knew that she could make more money as a migrant domestic worker than in a regular job in Indonesia. Grace was ambitious about making money. She invested the money that she earned into her business in Indonesia.

After working as a migrant domestic worker for more than ten years, Grace had already purchased a house for her mother in North Sulawesi and another house for herself and Sharon in Malang, Java (Sharon's hometown). Grace posted a picture of this house on Facebook with a caption "My project . . . and reason why I have to go back to Indonesia . . . home sweet home." From the picture, I saw that the house was still under construction and not ready for occupancy yet. In addition to buying a house in Malang, Grace also had a business there. Whenever Grace returned to Indonesia for her holiday, she went to Malang after visiting her mother in Sulawesi. Her business in Malang provided a good reason for her to frequent there. When Grace was in Malang, she visited Sharon's home and spent time with her two daughters, even though Sharon did not go on the trip. According to Grace, Sharon's two daughters were very close to her: the daughters called her "mommy"; she treated them as her own. To the two daughters who did not know the actual relationship between Grace and their mother, the word "mommy" may be *ibu*, which does not necessarily mean "mother" but is a respectful term for senior women in Indonesia. However, the word "mommy" indeed meant a lot to Grace, who psychologically considered Sharon's daughters her own. The first couple of times, I was confused by who Grace meant when she talked about "her daughters." Grace clarified that she was referring to Sharon's daughters.

Grace realized part of her imagined home by parenting Sharon's two daughters during her occasional visits. Her mommy-daughter relationship with Sharon's daughters *queered* the space of home as it challenged the logic of heteronormativity—the children have two mothers in a same-sex relationship.

Grace did many things to prepare herself to live in Malang; for example, operating a business and buying a house. However, both Grace and Sharon still worried about cohabiting in Indonesia. Sharon said that her mother still wants her to remarry. Indeed, her mother had arranged a fiancé for Sharon, but Sharon refused to marry him. Meanwhile, Grace believed that her natal family would challenge her if she moved to Malang permanently. She also worried that her father, who was a pastor, might intervene in her life if she returned home:

> My friends ask me why I am still working in Hong Kong since everything I own is in Indonesia. I ask them back what's good about going back to Indonesia. My family is very traditional as my dad is a pastor. I know I won't be able to do the things that I want to do if I go home.

Their anxieties, including the pressure on Sharon to remarry and the potential reaction of Grace's natal family, stopped them from carrying out a concrete plan for moving to Indonesia permanently. They did not know when a suitable time would be to return to Indonesia. One day, Grace posted a message on Facebook:

> Hong Kong is the best. Here, I have what I want . . . ambition and love . . . :-)
> [hkg the best . . . di sini q dapat apa yg ku mau . . . cita dan cinta . . . :-)]

The message suggested that Grace did not want to return to Indonesia any time soon. She wanted to stay in Hong Kong, which would allow her to pursue her ambition of making money and maintaining an intimate relationship with Sharon. She did not want her relocation to Malang to become a source of confrontation with her family. Therefore, Grace and Sharon remained in Hong Kong and continued to work as migrant domestic workers although they already had enough accumulated wealth for a decent life in Indonesia.

The two couples (Iman and Lestari, Grace and Sharon) fulfilled their same-sex desires by quietly remaking the space of home. They redefined the space of home by integrating their same-sex desires into the imagined home. Iman and Lestari became the husband and the wife of a new household; Grace showed her love to Sharon by parenting Sharon's two daughters. Mindful of upsetting their natal families, they decided to hide their romantic relationship under the guise of "sisterhood" and "deep friendship." Their imaginings and practices queered the space of home by subverting the heteronormative expectations without publicly rebelling against the marriage and family system.

Imagining the Future, Negotiating the Present

Not all Indonesian women in this study were comfortable with the idea of maintaining a same-sex relationship after returning to Indonesia. Among those who indicated that they would not continue their same-sex relationship after returning to Indonesia, all were unmarried, including seven *tomboi* and eight *cewek*. For these women, their imagined future emphasized the subject position of unmarried daughter and the expectation of marriage. Parker and Nilan (2013) noted that the expectation of marriage still holds true among the young generation in Indonesia, even though they expect to live modern, urban lives. According to Parker and Nilan, young Indonesians are embedded in their families and share their parents' belief that family is the heart of society. There are Islamists in Indonesia who consider the high number of unmarried women over the age of thirty to be problematic (Nurmila 2009). These Islamists perceive the rising age of marriage as the cause of more illicit extramarital sex (*zina*). Subject to the cultural norms and religious discourse, young women who are employed after graduation can negotiate when they marry; for example, they can postpone marriage to work for a few years (Naafs 2013). Although they can delay marriage, they are expected to marry before turning thirty. This is the context and cultural trajectory to explore how unmarried *cewek* and *tomboi* think about marriage and their future. How did their imagined future shape their practices and understanding of same-sex relationships in Hong Kong?

The unmarried *cewek* did not deny their desire for men. They dated men before they left for Hong Kong. Half (four of the eight unmarried *cewek*) currently had a boyfriend in Indonesia. Another two told me that they dated Indonesian men through online dating sites after they arrived in Hong Kong. However, both stopped dating men online because they found the relationships to be disappointing; the men already had a wife and children but claimed to be single. These two *cewek* started relationships with *tomboi* after joining pop dance groups.

In Indonesia, marriage and children are constructed as a rite of passage to womanhood. The unmarried *cewek* believed that marriage and children fit with their feminine identity. They eagerly looked forward to marriage. Michelle (thirty-two years old) was the oldest unmarried *cewek* in my study. She had been working as a migrant domestic worker for eight years. She did not have a boyfriend yet but was eager to marry. In her imagined future, Michelle had a family where she was a wife and mother:

> Because I am a woman, I want to get married. I really want it. Have my own family and kids. Really want it. Probably, now . . . but that seems so far away. The people around me are all women. [Karena saya perempuan, mau menikah. Saya pun ingin sekali. Punya keluarga, punya anak. Ingin banget. Mungkin, sekarang . . . jauh. Lingkungan saya semuanya cewek.]

Beby, who was twenty-four years old, shared a similar view. Beby had been working in Hong Kong for four years. She said that she would get married after returning to Indonesia.

> My family has already been pressuring me to go home and get married. But I'm afraid of going home now because I haven't saved up enough money yet. So, I don't think about getting married right now. And, I don't have a boyfriend yet.... I will earn and save money to get married so that my future husband and children will have a better life.

Beby said that the money she earned now was for a better life for her future husband and children. Her thought indicated a change in womanhood in today's Indonesia. While confined under a patriarchal culture, women, especially of the lower class, were expected to substantially contribute to the household economically by working overseas as domestic workers.

If these women imagined eventually marrying a man, what were their thoughts about their same-sex relationship in Hong Kong? As I discussed in Chapter 2, pop dance groups provided meanings by which the members could make sense of their same-sex relationship. When they left Hong Kong and the kin world of their pop dance group, the meanings of their same-sex relationship would change from marking them as "intelligible" to "unintelligible" persons in Indonesia. Therefore, they were determined to terminate their relationship after returning to Indonesia. They regarded their same-sex relationship as situational and only meaningful in the space of Hong Kong.

While unmarried *cewek* desired *tomboi* in Hong Kong, they were adamant that they did not want *tomboi* in Indonesia. The future in Indonesia was shaped by what they were doing in the present. They had struck a verbal agreement with their *tomboi* lover in Hong Kong. All of them told their *tomboi* lover that they would terminate the relationship after they returned home to Indonesia.

Michelle said that her *tomboi* lover (Eddy) had already agreed to separate when Michelle had to go home:

> I like being with Eddy because she is like a man who takes care of me. I feel good about this relationship because Eddy and I have already agreed that we begin in Hong Kong and end in Hong Kong. Later, after I go back to Indonesia, we will break up because I want to be with a man. I hope I can forget about being a lesbian when I am in Indonesia.

Sarah, who was twenty-six years old, also told Allen, her *tomboi* lover, that she would marry her fiancé in Indonesia and would not continue the relationship after marriage. I asked Sarah, whom she loved more, her fiancé or Allen. She told me:

> Now . . . [pausing and thinking for a short time] I think it's like half and half. Because my boyfriend [her fiancé] is for the rest of my life. Allen is only here.... Allen has a family too. She has a son. I can't see us continuing on [in

Indonesia]. I have to go home. I was honest with her and upfront with everything. She said that she was okay with it before we started [the relationship].

Michelle's and Sarah's narratives indicated how their imagination of the future shaped their practice of negotiating with their *tomboi* lover. Their desire to marry and have children in the future did not stop them from desiring *tomboi* in Hong Kong. At the same time, they were honest with their *tomboi* that they did not want to continue the relationship in Indonesia. They adopted the practice of establishing an agreement with their *tomboi* before starting the relationship. Through this agreement, the unmarried *cewek* managed the expectations of the *tomboi*, in affirming that the relationship was restricted to Hong Kong.

What were the effects of these verbal agreement on the women? While the purpose of managing the expectations of the *tomboi* is obvious, there was more to the agreement, as it provided a buffer zone for the women to explore and cultivate their desires for *tomboi* in Hong Kong. As Michelle said, she felt comfortable in her relationship with Eddy because she knew that her parents in Indonesia would never know about it. The future home the women imagined reflected their decision of terminating the same-sex relationships and then getting married after returning Indonesia. Nevertheless, the future home did not stop these women from desiring *tomboi* at the moment in Hong Kong. They continued this way of life and enjoyed the love and care provided by their *tomboi* in Hong Kong. They seemed to embody docility in fantasizing about the conventional life path of becoming a wife and then a mother. However, docility constituted only part of their sexual subjectivity. They did not restrict their desire and sexuality to marriage or to men only. Their sexual subjectivities emphasized the ideal path of marriage without sacrificing the pleasurable moments of their relationships with *tomboi* in Hong Kong.

Ambivalent Future

The *tomboi* who said that they would end up getting married after returning to Indonesia had ambivalent feelings about their future. They told me that they were not physical attracted to men. Although they dated boys during their school years, they claimed that they did not really like men. For instance, they would say that they did not let their former boyfriends kiss them but would always want to kiss and touch their girlfriends in Hong Kong. These *tomboi* did not show any eagerness for marriage, the path that they are expected to walk after returning to Indonesia.

The *tomboi* perceived marriage as a family obligation. They believed their parents would be upset if they refused to marry. A twenty-four-year-old *tomboi* shared her imagined future with me:

> I want to be with a woman, but I also want to make my mother happy. Later, I will be with a man if I go back to Indonesia. [Mau sama cewek, tapi aku juga mau ibuku senang. Jadi nanti harus sama cowok kalo pulang ke indo.]

The *tomboi* expressed ambivalent feelings about their future. They were caught in a dilemma between the expectation to marry, lack of desire for men, and by contrast, their desire for women. They therefore tried to avoid marriage by prolonging their stay in Hong Kong. Among the seven unmarried *tomboi*, six were under the age of thirty. They were able to postpone marriage and escape their future home by convincing their parents that they wanted to earn more money and had no plans for marriage.

This strategy of resistance works for younger *tomboi* but not for those who are already over thirty years old. Leo was already thirty-one at the time of my fieldwork and had been working in Hong Kong for nine years. She had three relationships with *cewek* in Hong Kong. She was heartbroken when her last girlfriend returned to Indonesia and married a man. Now, marriage was posing another challenge to her—recently, her mother asked her to return home and marry. She felt significantly pressured by her mother. Leo shared her ambivalent vision of the future:

> I call my mom once a week. Every time I call her, she asks me to go back to Indonesia and get married. Before, I had to send a lot of money home to my family. So, my mom did not ask me to go back. But [my family] has already bought a house. I also gave money to my younger brother to operate his own business. Another younger brother also finished school, which I paid for. He has a job now. My family does not need that much money from me. So, my mom always keeps asking me to go home. But I can't make up my mind. I keep asking myself, "Should I go home? What about my future? Should I marry some guy?" I haven't found anyone that I like yet. Actually, I have never been in love with any man. I am afraid of getting married. If I have to get married, I am afraid of not knowing how to get along with a man. I don't know anything about men. What will it be like if I'm in a relationship with a man?

I asked Leo whether her mother would arrange a marriage and force her to marry a man. Leo said:

> No, my mother would not do that to me. She said that I must be in love with the man. But my mother keeps asking me to go back to Indonesia. She said that it's hard to find a good man here [in Hong Kong].

I then asked Leo whether it would be possible to live apart from her parents in Indonesia. Leo replied:

> If I was in Jakarta, I think that would be possible. But you know, in Indonesia, if a girl doesn't live with her parents, people would talk behind her back and say things like, "She's a bad girl." If a girl is unmarried, she should live with her family.

Leo was wavering because on the one hand, she did not want to get married, but on the other hand, she could not find any more excuses to prolong her stay in Hong Kong when her duty of sending money back home was completed. She understood the goal of her migration to Hong Kong as only a sacrifice for her family rather than the pursuit of her own personal development. It was assumed that she would return home and marry when the mission was completed.

Leo was aware that she still had the power to refuse marriage by saying that she had not found a man whom she loves. She understood that her mother would not force her to marry otherwise. The idea of "romantic love," that a desirable marriage should be based on mutual love and passion, became popular in Indonesia after the 1970s, and Indonesian women have enjoyed increasing autonomy in choosing their marriage partner (Nurmila 2009). Leo was able to negotiate the postponement of marriage by manipulating the modern discourse of romantic love to which she was subject.

After several months, I called Leo and invited her to meet with me. The two of us went to a fast food shop in Causeway Bay. Leo told me that she had decided to return home after finishing her current contract, in another year. That day, I observed that she dressed differently and had changed from a *tomboi* style to a ladylike one. The first time that I saw Leo, she had short hair and wore a unisex athletic jacket, baggy jeans, and a pair of Converse sneakers. Leo had also grown out her hair, which was long enough to put in a ponytail. She mentioned her long hair: "My parents know that I am growing my hair. They are very happy. Knowing that they are happy, I am also very happy." Leo wore earrings, which were evident after she pulled her hair back into a ponytail. She wore a women's slim-fitting blouse instead of the athletic jacket. Her change in gender appearance was consistent with her plans to return home and marry. She was intent on finding a boyfriend in Indonesia, and so she changed her appearance to appeal more to men.

Leo's story demonstrates how unmarried *tomboi* negotiate their existence. Before the age of thirty, unmarried woman can delay marriage by using overseas employment as an excuse. Parents usually allow them to delay marriage because making money is their daughter's priority while working in Hong Kong. Therefore, parents do not insist that their daughter return home and marry. However, this strategy has its limitations. When a woman is over the age of thirty and has already fulfilled the obligation of financing the needs of her natal family, she faces increasing pressure to marry. Leo was over thirty and had already completed her obligation to support her two brothers financially. Leo's mother kept reminding her about the importance of marriage during their weekly telephone conversations. Her mother's ongoing persuasion compelled Leo to identify with the position of an unmarried woman as well as the desirable future of building a family with a man. Leo convinced herself and identified with this desirable future with a man.

Summary

This chapter has investigated the imaginings of home projected by Indonesian women while working in Hong Kong. Their imaginaries of their future home provide important information for understanding their desires and sexuality in relation to the local ideology of migration and marriage as well as the political economy of family, that is, the gender division of labor and the earnings contributed by women. The narratives of their future home reflect their desires, fears, confusion, and ambivalence; these emotions in turn inform and shape their sexual subjectivity—their identified gendered positions and how they address their same-sex relationship now and in the future.

To unravel the sexuality of migrant women in a transnational context, the ways that they obtained knowledge through the contacts and transactions of their travel across Indonesia and Hong Kong has been examined. Labor migration provided these women with not only monetary reward but also exposure to big cities and the opportunity to accumulate cultural capital. The benefits and resources that these women earned in the migratory process enabled them to imagine a future home with a female lover. The imaginaries of their future home provided motivation and meanings for them to continue their work in Hong Kong. That is, they needed a substantial amount of funds to start a new life in the cities of Indonesia.

The chapter also enriches the notion of Asian queer subjectivity by addressing how Indonesian women insinuated their homoerotic desires into the heteronormative logic of home. Their sexual subjectivity was filled with both same-sex desires and heteronormative practices. They were mindful of upsetting their harmonic relationship with their parents, so they applied the heteronormative expectations of sisterhood and mutual help between close friends to camouflage their same-sex relationship. Their same-sex relationships quietly remade the space of home. That is, they redefined their family positions in accordance with their new gender (*tomboi* or *cewek*); they established a home with two mommies by parenting their girlfriend's children.

Addressing the Islamic context where parents closely monitor the sexuality of their daughters, this chapter has also attended to the women who would not continue a same-sex relationship after returning to their natal family. They imagined that they would eventually marry. However, their imaginary did not suppress or stop their same-sex desire; they maximized their romantic and sexual enjoyment with women when they were still in Hong Kong. Their seemingly docile bodies on the one hand, complied with family expectations but on the other hand, exhibited autonomy and agency to enjoy homoerotic relationships, at least in the space of Hong Kong.

Conclusion

Bridging Asian Labor Migration with Queer Studies

When I first started this research project in 2008, I received some discouraging feedback. One criticism was that focus of the research project was overly narrow, that I was addressing the sexuality of only migrant domestic workers. The niche may be small and appear insignificant; however, it can have significant implications, as it renders two distinctively different areas of studies mutually relevant, bridging Asian labor migration studies and lesbian and queer studies. Using an ethnographic approach, I delved into the struggles and concerns of these Indonesian women and examined their changing notions of gender, sexuality, family, and marriage in the migratory process.

My study of the same-sex desires and practices of these Indonesian women has broadened and enriched the scholarship of Asian labor migration, creating representation for migrant workers who are not satisfied with confinement to the roles of wife and mother. My work responds to the call of Martin Manalansan (2006) to go beyond the heteronormative assumptions evident in the scholarship of transnational family and motherhood. The Indonesian women in this study do not necessarily abandon their traditional roles, because some of them claim that they are prepared to marry after returning to Indonesia. Nevertheless, they show their intentionality and become sexual agents during their stay in Hong Kong. They produce gender/sexual knowledge by circulating stories about *tomboi* and love-making scenes at the training centers, as well as depicting biological men as greedy and unfaithful. They participate in daily interactions, Sunday activities, and celebration rituals that make same-sex relationships between Indonesian women legitimate and desirable.

This ethnographic study of the same-sex desires of Indonesian women expands the academic discussion of queer people in Asia. The book has vividly shown how these women evaluate their same-sex relationships in Hong Kong in relation to Indonesian ideologies and the political economy of family. Possessing financial resources and overseas exposure, these Indonesian women earn more power in negotiating expectations with their parents, such as the timing of marriage and the selection of a spouse. Their enhanced autonomy enables them to worry less about their traditional roles and to explore things that are inconceivable to them in Indonesia. Unlike their Western counterparts, Indonesian women have strong family ties and are not supposed to leave their parents before getting married. They improvise strategies that help to manage this marriage pressure and the homophobic atmosphere in Indonesian homes and communities.

In addition, this book enriches Asian queer studies, as it documents the contingent view of gender adopted by these Indonesian women. They are subjected to a seemingly "either *tomboi* or *cewek*" gender system, in which the boundaries are clearly marked in terms of clothing, hairstyle, and roles in a relationship. Pop dance groups are not only their platform to showcase their talent and fashion sense but arenas for learning and expressing their gender identification. For instance, the two genders have been institutionalized in the fashion shows. The attributes of these two genders are clearly marked and differentiated. Plus, the kin relations established among the pop dance group members clearly indicate the gender of every individual, *tomboi* or *cewek*, as well as seniority in the group. These Indonesian women act in accordance with their kin position in the group and follow the gendered expectations in order to become intelligible persons.

For them, gender is not biologically determined but refers to a set of gendered activities and everyday practices, such as the act of pampering and being pampered in a relationship between a *tomboi* and a *cewek*. I relied on the concept of intersubjectivity in Moore (1994) to explain how the identity of the Indonesian women as *tomboi* or *cewek* result from being positioned as *tomboi* or *cewek* by others. My findings also reveal the flexibility of the "*tomboi/cewek*" gender system, which allows a person to shift to the opposite gender to ensure that the same-sex relationship is composed of two genders. The change is intelligible because these Indonesian women value the intelligibility of the same-sex relationship, which consists of one *tomboi* and one *cewek*, more than the consistency of self-identification (*tomboi* or *cewek*). While Butler (1999) argues that intelligibility results from maintaining a coherent relationship to one's culturally defined sex, gender, and desire—that is, what she calls the matrix of intelligibility—my work suggests that gender and desire are not necessarily equally weighted in the matrix of intelligibility. I argue that the relationship between gender and desire is not fixed but contingent on wider social relations, such as the kin world of these Indonesian women. By viewing gender expression in relation to the interaction between individuals and their communities, rather than solely as a matter of self-discovery, this book underscores the contingency of gender expression, especially in the context of migration, when individuals are away from familiar social contexts and exposed to new discourses and desires.

By including low-skilled Asian female migrant workers in queer studies or in other words, by situating women's same-sex desires and practices in a labor migratory context, this book shows the shifting boundaries of heteronormativity and how these boundaries are shaped by different parties in both Indonesia and Hong Kong, including the government bodies, employment agents, Hong Kong people, media, and religious groups. The moral discourse of migration and its heteronormative expectations sometimes cause dilemmas for these women. Chapter 3 addresses how Indonesian women produce the notion of *cuma di sini* (only here) when they are on the one hand being encouraged to work overseas but on the other hand have no choice but to violate religious taboos, as their Hong Kong employers require them to touch pork or forbid them from praying. This notion unexpectedly enables these women to justify and even reconcile the conflict between Islam and their lesbian practices. Their views of religious piety gradually transform as migration distances them from home and religion. These Indonesian women are then able to generate a rather positive view of same-sex relationships when Islamic principles are no longer absolute rules but negotiable depending on the situation and context. Furthermore, the notorious requests and rules of Hong Kong employers as well as the business owners of karaoke boxes and rental rooms also produce a discourse in which migrant women should neither dress to appeal men nor spend time with men on Sundays; proper women gather only with other women. The requests and rules produce a homosocial environment for these Indonesian women, whose same-sex relationships are left unmarked and are therefore tolerated.

Transnational Sexuality: The Present and the Future

This ethnographic study unravels the sexuality of migrant women in a transnational context. Traveling between Indonesia and Hong Kong, their movement not only provides monetary reward but also produces knowledge that constitutes their new views on gender, sexuality, religion, and their future home as well as confers skills that enhance their cultural capital for survival in the cities of Indonesia. About half of the Indonesian women in this study project their future home with a same-sex partner after returning to Indonesia. The knowledge and contacts that these women have obtained in the process of labor migration have exceeded their expectations prior to leaving home.

The significance of examining these migrant women's imaginings of home is that it reveals the intertwining relationship between the present and the future: same-sex desires and practices in Hong Kong and their imagined home in Indonesia. Whether these women strive toward or achieve their imagined home is the least concern of this research project. As I have shown in the previous chapters, sexuality is fluid and can be changed in different contexts and situations. These migrant women might change their mind after they actually return to Indonesia. Some couples have already parted ways as I write this conclusion. Nevertheless, these changes do not undermine the findings of the project because the purpose of examining their imaginings of home is to provide a transnational perspective so as to broaden the notion of sexuality by taking the Indonesian ideologies of gender, sexuality, and marriage into account even while the women remain overseas. Their imaginings of home help us to rethink sexuality as an ongoing process of negotiation between the present and the future and between the local ideologies and imaginations in a globalizing world.

The books sheds light on the meanings of same-sex relationships to Indonesian women. Instead of searching for reasons to explain *why* they engage in a same-sex relationship, such as loneliness or lack of men in their social circle, this book provides an ethnographic perspective by addressing their activities during the migratory process and considering how the policies and rules of different parties shape as well as transform the meanings of same-sex relationships for these migrant women. The Indonesian women in this study do not see sexuality as a fixed identity. Instead, their views on and understanding of their same-sex desires and practices shift according to context. Situated in the pop dance groups (Chapter 2), they are prompted to view same-sex relationships as appealing and desirable. Or when they can imagine a happy future with their same-sex lover, for example, settling in a city and running a small business together (Chapter 4), they consider their same-sex relationship add meaning to their lives. However, when they are persuaded or pressured by their parents to return home, they view same-sex relationships as problematic and taboo after returning to Indonesia. Therefore, the question of what a same-sex relationship means to these women is subject to change when the women encounter different situations, including both opportunities and limitations, in the present and in the future.

Maid to Queer

Intentionally focusing on migrant domestic workers who come from a heterosexual background, this book provides an intersectional lens for understanding the feminization of international migration as well as the transformations of the structural constraints imposed on maids that unintentionally become productive possibilities of queerness and normativity. Feminization of international migration has contributed to the emergence of single-sex migrant communities in which Indonesian men are mostly absent; additionally, the huge income gap between women who work in Hong Kong and men who are left in Indonesia also makes these women skeptical and distrustful of men.

Following heteronormative logic, the Indonesian women in this study are able to produce and experience possibilities that were inconceivable before leaving home. They make sense of new gender categories (*tomboi* and *cewek*) and establish a "hierarchy of good women" with an emphasis on good labor and changing definitions of Islamic piety taught by their parents and the employment agencies. Maids are never docile bodies; their queer desires do not constrain them from reentering the heterosexual world in the future.

Addressing the changes from maid to queer, this book enriches both Asian labor migration and queer studies by documenting the intersections of domestic work, labor migration, race, and religion on the sexual subject formation. *Maid to Queer* documents how Indonesian migrant women reconstitute normativity and remake a space for their love, sex, and intimacy without publicly upsetting heteronormativity.

References

Allard, Tom, and Wilda Asmarini. 2018. "Indonesian President Picks Cleric as Running Mate for Election." *Reuters*, August 9. Accessed May 29, 2019. https://www.reuters.com/article/us-indonesia-politics/indonesian-president-picks-cleric-as-running-mate-for-election-idUSKBN1KU0JF.

Amaria, Lola, dir. 2010. *Minggu Pagi di Victoria Park*. Pic[k] Lock Productions, Indonesia.

AMC (Asian Migrant Centre), IMWU (Indonesian Migrant Workers Union), and KOTKIHO (The Hong Kong Coalition of Indonesian Migrant Workers Organization). 2007. *Underpayment 2: The Continuing Systematic Extortion of Indonesian Domestic Workers in Hong Kong; An In-Depth Study of Indonesian Labor Migration in Hong Kong*. Hong Kong: AMC.

Anggraeni, Dewi. 2006. *Dreamseekers: Indonesian Women as Domestic Workers in Asia*. Jakarta: Equinox.

Appadurai, Arjun. 1996. *Modernity at Large: Cultural Dimensions of Globalization*. Vol. 1, *Public Worlds*. Minneapolis: University of Minnesota Press.

Appadurai, Arjun 2002. "Disjuncture and Difference in the Global Cultural Economy." In *The Anthropology of Globalization: A Reader*, edited by Jonathan Xavier Inda and Renato Rosaldo, 46–64. Malden, MA: Blackwell.

Apple Daily. 2013. "男僱主圖「拗直」印傭" [Male employer attempts to "cure" Indonesian worker]. November 9. Accessed April 26, 2014. http://hk.apple.nextmedia.com/news/art/20131109/18500230.

Apple Daily. 2014a. "印傭同志媽媽「我不需要男人」" [Indonesian worker lesbian mother: "I don't need men"]. February 14. Accessed April 26, 2014. http://hk.apple.nextmedia.com/news/art/20140214/18625612.

Apple Daily. 2014b. "我是僱主 我接受印傭同志" [I am an employer I accept lesbian Indonesian workers], February 14. Accessed April 26, 2014. http://hk.apple.nextmedia.com/news/art/20140214/18625614.

Arum, Pandan. 2010. "Cinta Sejenis yang Mengakibatkan Aku Radang Usus" [Same-sex love that caused me enteritis]. *Pandu: Manuju BMI Mandiri & Berprestasi* [Guide: Indonesian migrant workers toward independence and achievement], November.

Bailey, Marlon M. 2011. "Gender/Racial Realness: Theorizing the Gender System in Ballroom Culture." *Feminist Studies* 37 (2): 365–86.

Bailey, Marlon M. 2013. *Butch Queens Up in Pumps: Gender, Performance, and Ballroom Culture in Detroit*. Ann Arbor: University of Michigan Press.

Barth, Thomas. 2012. "Relationships and Sexuality of Imprisoned Men in the German Penal System: A Survey of Inmates in a Berlin Prison." *International Journal of Law and Psychiatry* 35: 153–58.

Bastide, Loïs. 2015. "Faith and Uncertainty: Migrants' Journeys between Indonesia, Malaysia and Singapore." *Health, Risk & Society* 17 (3–4): 226–45.

BBC. 2019. "Indonesia Election: Joko Widodo Re-elected as President." May 21. Accessed May 29, 2019. https://www.bbc.com/news/world-asia-48331879.

Bennett, Linda Rae. 2005. *Women, Islam and Modernity: Single Women, Sexuality and Reproduction Health in Contemporary Indonesia*. New York: Routledge.

Bennett, Linda Rae. 2008. "Poverty, Opportunity and Purity in Paradise: Women Working in Lombok's Tourist Hotels." In *Women and Work in Indonesia*, edited by Michele Ford and Lyn Parker, 82–103. London: Routledge.

Blackwood, Evelyn. 1995. "Falling in Love with An-Other Lesbian: Reflections on Identity in Fieldwork." In *Taboo: Sex, Identity and Erotic Subjectivity in Anthropological Fieldwork*, edited by Don Kulick and Margaret Willson, 39–57. London: Routledge.

Blackwood, Evelyn. 2007. "Regulation of Sexuality in Indonesian Discourse: Normative Gender, Criminal Law and Shifting Strategies of Control." *Culture, Health & Sexuality* 9 (3): 293–307.

Blackwood, Evelyn. 2010. *Falling into the Lesbi World: Desire and Difference in Indonesia*. Honolulu: University of Hawai'i Press.

Blackwood, Evelyn, and Mark Johnson. 2012. "Queer Asian Subjects: Transgressive Sexualities and Heteronormative Meanings." *Asian Studies Review* 36 (4): 441–51. https://doi.org/10.1080/10357823.2012.741037.

Blackwood, Evelyn, and Saskia E. Wieringa, eds. 1999. *Female Desires: Same-Sex Relations and Transgender Practices across Cultures*. New York: Columbia University Press.

Blackwood, Evelyn, and Saskia E. Wieringa. 2007. "Globalization, Sexuality, and Silences: Women's Sexualities and Masculinities in an Asian Context." In *Women's Sexualities and Masculinities in a Globalizing Asia*, edited by Saskia Wieringa, Evelyn Blackwood, and Abha Bhaiya, 1–20. New York: Palgrave Macmillan.

Boellstorff, Tom. 1999. "The Perfect Path: Gay Men, Marriage, Indonesia." *GLQ: A Journal of Lesbian and Gay Studies* 5 (4): 475–510.

Boellstorff, Tom. 2004a. "The Emergence of Political Homophobia in Indonesia: Masculinity and National Belonging." *Ethnos* 69 (4): 465–86.

Boellstorff, Tom. 2004b. "Zines and Zones of Desire: Mass-Mediated Love, National Romance, and Sexual Citizenship in Gay Indonesia." *Journal of Asian Studies* 63(2): 367–402.

Boellstorff, Tom. 2007. "Queer Studies in the House of Anthropology." *Annual Review of Anthropology* 36 (1): 17–35. https://doi.org/10.1146/annurev.anthro.36.081406.094421.

Boellstorff, Tom. 2016. "Against State Straightism: Five Principles for Including LGBT Indonesians." E-Internatiomal Relations, March 21, 2016. Accessed October 10, 2016. http://www.e-ir.info/2016/03/21/against-state-straightism-five-principles-for-including-lgbt-indonesians/.

Borch, Rosslyn von der. 2008. "Straddling Worlds: Indonesian Migrant Domestic Workers in Singapore." In *Women and Work in Indonesia*, edited by Michele Ford and Lyn Parker, 195–214. London: Routledge.

Bourdieu, Pierre. 1990. *The Logic of Practice*. Stanford, CA: Stanford University Press.

Brenner, Suzanne. 1996. "Reconstructing Self and Society: Javanese Muslim Women and 'the Veil.'" *American Ethnologist* 23 (4): 673–97.

Brenner, Suzanne. 2005. "Islam and Gender Politics in Late New Order Indonesia." In *Spirited Politics: Religion and Public Life in Contemporary Southeast Asia*, edited by Andrew C. Willford and Kenneth M. George. Ithaca, NY: Southeast Asia Program, Cornell University.

Brenner, Suzanne. 2011. "Private Moralities in the Public Sphere: Democratization, Islam, and Gender in Indonesia." *American Anthropologist* 113 (3): 478–90.

Butler, Judith. 1999. *Gender Trouble: Feminism and the Subversion of Identity*. 10th Anniversary Edition. New York: Routledge.

Cantú, Lionel, Jr. 2009. *The Sexuality of Migration: Border Crossings and Mexican Immigrant Men*. Edited by Nancy A. Naples and Salvador Vidal-Ortiz. New York: New York University Press.

Carillo, Hector. 2004. "Sexual Migration, Cross-Cultural Sexual Encounters, and Sexual Health." *Sexuality Research and Social Policy* 1 (3): 58–70.

Census and Statistics Department, Government of the Hong Kong Special Administrative Region. 2018a. "Labour Force Characteristics." Accessed June 2, 2019. https://www.censtatd.gov.hk/hkstat/sub/gender/labour_force/index.jsp.

Census and Statistics Department, Government of the Hong Kong Special Administrative Region. 2018b. "Population." Accessed June 2, 2019. https://www.censtatd.gov.hk/hkstat/sub/so20.jsp.

Chan, Carol. 2016. "In Sickness and In Wealth." *Inside Indonesia*, January 9. Accessed May 3, 2017. http://www.insideindonesia.org/in-sickness-and-in-wealth?highlight=WyJpbiIsIidpbiIsIidpbiciLCInaW4nLCIsImluJy4iLCJzaWNrbmVzcyIsIidzaWNrbmVzcyIsIiwiaW4gc2lja25lc3MiXQ%3D%3D.

Cho, Man Kit, Lucetta Yip Lo Kam, and Francisca Yuenki Lai. 2018. "千禧年後的香港同志運動圖像：連結、衝突和限制" [Hong Kong's LGBT movement after the millennium: Alliance, conflict, and limitation]. In 社運年代：香港抗爭政治的軌跡 [An epoch of social movements: The trajectory of contentious politics in Hong Kong], edited by Wai Edmund Cheng and Wai Hei Samson Yuen, 115–40. Hong Kong: Chinese University Press.

Constable, Nicole. 1997. *Maid to Order in Hong Kong: Stories of Filipina Workers*. Ithaca, NY: Cornell University Press.

Constable, Nicole. 2000. "Dolls, T-Birds and Ideal Workers: The Negotiation of Filipino Identity in Hong Kong." In *Home and Hegemony: Domestic Service and Identity Politics in South and Southeast Asia*, edited by Kathleen M. Adams and Sara Dickey, 221–47. Ann Arbor: University of Michigan Press.

Constable, Nicole. 2002. "Filipina Workers in Hong Kong Homes: Household Rules and Relations." In *Global Woman: Nannies, Maids, and Sex Workers in the New Economy*, edited by Barbara Ehrenreich and Arlie Russell Hochschild, 115–41. New York: Henry Holt.

Constable, Nicole. 2010. "Migrant Workers and the Many States of Protest in Hong Kong." In *Migrant Workers in Asia: Distant Divides, Intimate Connections*, edited by Nicole Constable, 127–44. London: Routledge.

Constable, Nicole. 2011. "Telling Tales of Migrant Workers in Hong Kong: Transformations of Faith, Life Scripts, and Activism." In *Diasporic Journeys, Ritual, and Normativity among Asian Migrant Women*, edited by Pnina Werbner and Mark Johnson, 107–25. London: Routledge.

Constable, Nicole. 2014. *Born out of Place: Migrant Mothers and the Politics of International Labor*. Hong Kong: Hong Kong University Press.

Daily Mail Online. 2017. "Indonesian Police Arrest 141 Men including One Briton for Holding a 'Gay Sex Party' at a Sauna in the Country's Latest Crackdown on Homosexuality." May 23. Accessed May 29, 2019. http://www.dailymail.co.uk/news/article-4529014/Indonesian-police-make-mass-arrests-gay-party.html.

Davies, Sharyn Graham. 2010. *Gender Diversity in Indonesia: Sexuality, Islam and Queer Selves*. London: Routledge.

Davies, Sharyn Graham. 2016. "Indonesia's Anti-LGBT Panic." East Asia Forum. Accessed May 26, 2019. http://www.eastasiaforum.org/2016/07/15/indonesias-anti-lgbt-panic/.

Diamond, Lisa M. 2008. *Sexual Fluidity: Understanding Women's Love and Desire*. Cambridge, MA: Harvard University Press.

Dubisch, Jill. 1995. "Lovers in the Field: Sex, Dominance, and the Female Anthropologist." In *Taboo: Sex, Identity, and Erotic Subjectivity in Anthropological Fieldwork*, edited by Don Kulick and Margaret Willson, 29–50. London: Routledge.

Duggan, Lisa. 2002. "The New Homonormativity: The Sexual Politics of Neoliberalism." In *Materializing Democracy: Toward a Revitalized Cultural Politics*, edited by Russ Castronovo and Dana D. Nelson, 175–94. Durham, NC: Duke University Press.

Ehrenreich, Barbara, and Arlie Russell Hochschild, eds. 2002. *Global Woman: Nannies, Maids, and Sex Workers in the New Economy*. New York: Metropolitan Books.

Elias, Juanita. 2013. "The State and the Foreign Relations of Households: The Malaysia-Indonesia Domestic Worker Dispute " In *The Global Political Economy of the Household in Asia*, edited by Samanthi J. Gunawardana and Juanita Elias. Hampshire: Palgrave Macmillan.

Elmhirst, Rebecca. 2007. "Tigers and Gangsters: Masculinities and Feminised Migration in Indonesia." *Population, Space and Place* 13: 225–38.

Engebretsen, Elisabeth L. 2014. *Queer Women in Urban China: An Ethnography*. New York: Routledge.

Erel, Umut. 2010. "Migrating Cultural Capital: Bourdieu in Migration Studies." *Sociology* 44 (4): 642–60.

Espín, Oliva M. 1996. "The Immigrant Experience in Lesbian Studies." In *The New Lesbian Studies: Into the Twenty-First Century*, edited by Bonnie Zimmerman and Toni McNaron, 79–85. New York: Feminist Press at the City University of New York.

Ford, Michele, and Lenore Lyons. 2008. "Making the Best of What You've Got: Sex Work and Class Mobility in the Riau Islands." In *Women and Work in Indonesia*, edited by Michele Ford and Lyn Parker, 173–94. London: Routledge.

Fortier, Anne-Marie. 2001. "'Coming Home': Queer Migrations and Multiple Evocations of Home." *European Journal of Cultural Studies* 4 (4): 405–24.

Foucault, Michel. 1984. *The Foucault Reader*. Edited by Paul Rainbow. London: Penguin Books.

Gopinath, Gayatri. 2005. *Impossible Desires: Queer Diasporas and South Asian Public Cultures*. Durham, NC: Duke University Press.

Government of the Hong Kong Special Administrative Region. 2005. "The Rights of the Individual: Equal Opportunities. Accessed April 26, 2014." Last modified 2013. http://www.cmab.gov.hk/en/issues/equal.htm.

Government of the Hong Kong Special Administrative Region. 2019. "Press Releases: Minimum Allowable Wage and Food Allowance for Foreign Domestic Helpers to Increase." Accessed June 24, 2019. https://www.info.gov.hk/gia/general/201809/28/P2018092800357.htm?fontSize=1.

Grewal, Inderpal, and Caren Kaplan. 2001. "Global Identities: Theorizing Transnational Studies of Sexuality." *GLQ: Journal of Lesbian and Gay Studies* 7 (4): 663–79.

Herek, Gregory M. 2012. "Facts about Homosexuality and Mental Health." Accessed May 28, 2019. https://psychology.ucdavis.edu/rainbow/html/facts_mental_health.html.

HK01. 2016. "驚老公出軌 女僱主偏向請女同志外傭 平權組織：性向是兩刃刀" [Worrying that husbands would have affairs female employers prefer lesbian workers LGBT groups: Sexual orientation is a double-edged sword], March 1. Accessed June 5, 2017. https://www.hk01.com/%E6%B8%AF%E8%81%9E/9291/%E9%A9%9A%E8%80%81%E5%85%AC%E5%87%BA%E8%BB%8C-%E5%A5%B3%E5%83%B1%E4%B8%BB%E5%81%8F%E5%90%91%E8%AB%8B%E5%A5%B3%E5%90%8C%E5%BF%97%E5%A4%96%E5%82%AD-%E5%B9%B3%E6%AC%8A%E7%B5%84%E7%B9%94-%E6%80%A7%E5%90%91%E6%98%AF%E5%85%A9%E5%88%83%E5%88.

HK01. 2018. "同志遊行1.2萬人創新高" [12,000 attended Pride Parade]. November 17. Accessed 31 May 2019. https://www.hk01.com/%E7%A4%BE%E6%9C%83%E6-%96%B0%E8%81%9E/260352/%E5%90%8C%E5%BF%97%E9%81%8A%E8%A1%8C-1-2%E8%90%AC%E4%BA%BA%E5%89%B5%E6%96%B0%E9%AB%98-%E9%BB%83%E8%80%80%E6%98%8E-%E5%A4%A7%E7%9C%BE%E5%8B%BF%E9%81%BF%E8%AB%87%E5%90%8C%E6%80%A7%E5%A9%9A%E5%A7%BB.

Hoang, Lan Anh, and Brenda S. A. Yeoh. 2015. "'I'd Do It for Love or for Money': Vietnamese Women in Taiwan and the Social Construction of Female Migrant Sexuality." *Gender, Place and Culture: A Journal of Feminist Geography* 22 (5): 591–607.

Home Affairs Bureau, Hong Kong Special Administrative Region. 2005. *Your Guide to Services in Hong Kong*. Accessed July 21, 2018. http://www.hab.gov.hk/file_manager/en/documents/references/papers_reports_others/equal_opportunities/Engversion4thMastercopy.pdf.

Hong Kong Pride Parade. 2016. "History." Accessed May 23, 2017. http://www.hkpride.net/2016/en/history.html.

Hong Kong Pride Parade. 2018. "History." Accessed May 31, 2019. https://hkpride.net/hk/history/.

House News. 2014. "專訪在港印尼女同志" [An interview with Indonesian lesbians in Hong Kong], January 3.

Human Rights Watch. 2017a. "Indonesia: 'Gay Porn' Arrests Threaten Privacy; Discriminatory Raid May Bring 15-Year Prison Terms." May 4. Accessed May 14, 2017. https://www.hrw.org/news/2017/05/04/indonesia-gay-porn-arrests-threaten-privacy.

Human Rights Watch. 2017b. "Indonesia: Stop Raids on Homes of 'Suspected Lesbians.'" September 5. Accessed May 25, 2019. https://www.hrw.org/news/2017/09/05/indonesia-stop-raids-homes-suspected-lesbians.

Human Rights Watch. 2018. "Indonesia: Vice Presidential Candidate Has Anti-Rights Record." August 10. Accessed May 29, 2019. https://www.hrw.org/news/2018/08/10/indonesia-vice-presidential-candidate-has-anti-rights-record.

Hutton, Jeffrey. 2017. "Indonesian Constitutional Court Declines to Ban Sex Outside Marriage." *New York Times*, December 14, 2017.

International Organization for Migration. 2010. *Labour Migration From Indonesia: An Overview of Indonesian Migration to Selected Destinations in Asia and the Middle East*. Jakarta: International Organization for Migration.

Jackson, Stevi. 2006. "Gender, Sexuality and Heterosexuality: The Complexity (and Limits) of Heteronormativity." *Feminist Theory* 7 (1): 105–21.

Jakarta Post. 2016a. "Government Drafts Ban on LGBT Websites." March 5. Accessed May 26, 2019. https://www.thejakartapost.com/news/2016/03/05/government-drafts-ban-lgbt-websites.html.

Jakarta Post. 2016b. "Indonesian Psychiatrists Label LGBT as Mental Disorders." February 24. Accessed May 26, 2019. https://www.thejakartapost.com/news/2016/02/24/indonesian-psychiatrists-label-lgbt-mental-disorders.html.

Jakarta Post. 2016c. "Lawmaker Supports Broadcasting Commission's Prohibition of 'Feminine Men.'" March 1. Accessed May 26, 2019. https://www.thejakartapost.com/news/2016/03/01/lawmaker-supports-broadcasting-commission-s-prohibition-feminine-men.html.

Jakarta Post. 2016d. "LGBT Not Welcome at University: Minister." January 25, 2016. Accessed May 26, 2019. https://www.thejakartapost.com/news/2016/01/25/lgbt-not-welcome-university-minister.html.

Jones, Carla. 2007. "Fashion and Faith in Urban Indonesia." *Fashion Theory* 11 (2/3): 211–32.

Khanis, Suvianita. 2013. "Human Rights and the LGBTI Movement in Indonesia." *Journal of Women's Studies* 19 (1): 127–38, 147–48.

Kholifah, Ruby. 2006. "Sexuality in *Pesantren*: Discourses on Sexuality and the Personal Experiences of Female *Santri*." *Pakistan Journal of Women's Studies: Alam-e-Niswan* 13 (2): 201–14.

Killias, Olivia 2018. *Follow the Maid: Domestic Worker Migration in and from Indonesia*. Copenhagen: NIAS Press.

Kong, Travis S. K. 2010. *Chinese Male Homosexualities: Memba, Tongzhi and Golden Boy*. London: Routledge

Kong, Travis S. K., Sky H. L. Lau, and Eva C. Y. Li. 2015. "The Fourth Wave? A Critical Reflection on the *Tongzhi* Movement in Hong Kong" In *Routledge Handbook of Sexuality Studies in East Asia*, edited by Mark McLelland and Vera Mackie, 188–201. London: Routledge.

Kulick, Don. 1995. "Introducton: The Sexual Life of Anthropologists; Erotic Subjectivity and Ethnographic Work." In *Taboo: Sex, Identity, and Erotic Subjectivity in Anthropological Fieldwork*, edited by Don Kulick and Margaret Willson, 1–28. London: Routledge.

Lai, Francisca Yuenki. 2018a. "Migrant and Lesbian Activism: A Critical Review of Grassroots Politics." *Asian Anthropology* 17 (2): 135–50.

Lai, Francisca Yuenki. 2018b. "Sexuality at Imagined Home: Same-Sex Desires among Indonesian Migrant Domestic Workers in Hong Kong." *Sexualities* 21 (5–6): 899–913.

Lai, Ming-yan. 2010. "Dancing to Different Tunes: Performance and Activism among Migrant Domestic Workers in Hong Kong." *Women's Studies International Forum* 33: 501–11.

References

Lan, Pei-Chia. 2006. *Global Cinderellas: Migrant Domestics and Newly Rich Employers in Taiwan*. Durham, NC: Duke University Press.

Lau, Chris. 2018. "'Giant Step Forward for Equality' in Hong Kong as Same-Sex Couples Win Right to Spousal Visas in Court of Final Appeal." *South China Morning Post*, July 4. Accessed June 1, 2019. https://www.scmp.com/news/hong-kong/hong-kong-law-and-crime/article/2153682/top-hong-kong-court-rules-favour-lesbian.

Legislative Council Secretariat. 2017a. *Foreign Domestic Helpers and Evolving Care Duties in Hong Kong*. Accessed February 20, 2018. http://www.legco.gov.hk/research-publications/english/1617rb04-foreign-domestic-helpers-and-evolving-care-duties-in-hong-kong-20170720-e.pdf.

Legislative Council Secretariat. 2017b. *Religious Facilities in Hong Kong*. Accessed July 14, 2018. https://www.legco.gov.hk/research-publications/english/1718fs01-religious-facilities-in-hong-kong-20171208-e.pdf.

Lewin, Ellen. 2016. "Who's Queer? What's Queer? Queer Anthropology through the Lens of Ethnography." *Cultural Anthropology* 31 (4): 598–606.

Lewin, Ellen, and William L. Leap. 1996. Introduction to *Out in the Field: Reflections of Lesbian and Gay Anthropologists*, edited by Ellen Lewin and William L. Leap, 1–28. Urbana: University of Illinois Press.

Lewis, Nathaniel M. 2012. "Remapping Disclosure: Gay Men's Segmented Journeys of Moving Out and Coming Out." *Social and Cultural Geography* 13 (3): 211–31.

Liang, Li-Fang. 2011. "The Making of an 'Ideal' Live-in Migrant Care Worker: Recruiting, Training, Matching and Disciplining." *Ethnic and Racial Studies* 34 (11): 1815–34. https://doi.org/10.1080/01419870.2011.554571.

Lindquist, Johan. 2009a. *The Anxieties of Mobility: Migration and Tourism in the Indonesian Borderlands*. Honolulu: University of Hawai'i Press.

Lindquist, Johan. 2009b. "Petugas Lapangan, Field Agent." In "Figures of Indonesian Modernity," edited by Joshua Barker and Johan Lindquist. *Indonesia* 87 (April): 55–57.

Lindquist, Johan. 2018. "Infrastructures of Escort: Transnational Migration and Economies of Connection in Indonesia." *Indonesia* 105 (April): 77–95.

Luibhéid, Eithne. 2008. Introduction to "Queer/Migration: An Unruly Body of Scholarship." Special issue, *GLQ: A Journal of Lesbian and Gay Studies* 14 (2/3): 169–90. https://doi.org/10.1215/10642684-2007-029.

Mahy, Petra, Monika Swasti Winarnita, and Nicholas Herriman. 2016. "Presumptions of Promiscuity: Reflections on Being a Widow or Divorcee from Three Indonesian Communities." *Indonesia and the Malay World* 44 (128): 47–67. https://doi.org/10.1080/13639811.2015.1100872.

Manalansan, Martin F., IV. 2002. "A Queer Itinerary: Deviant Excursions into Modernities." In *Out in Theory: The Emergence of Lesbian and Gay Anthropology*, edited by Ellen Lewin and William L. Leap, 246–63. Urbana: University of Illinois Press.

Manalansan, Martin F., IV. 2003. *Global Divas: Filipino Gay Men in the Diaspora*. Durham, NC: Duke University Press.

Manalansan, Martin F., IV. 2006. "Queer Intersections: Sexuality and Gender in Migration Studies." *International Migration Review* 40 (1): 224–49.

Manalansan, Martin F., IV. 2018. "Messing Up Sex: The Promises and Possibilities of Queer of Color Critique." *Sexualities* 21 (8): 1287–90.

Mathews, Gordon. 2011. *Ghetto at the Center of the World: Chungking Mansions, Hong Kong*. Hong Kong: Hong Kong University Press.

Merigo, Eduard. 2019. "In Indonesia, LGBT Communities Viewed as a Moral Threat—Condemned by Religion and, Increasingly, by Law." *South China Morning Post*, April 7. Accessed May 26, 2019. https://www.scmp.com/magazines/post-magazine/long-reads/article/3004634/indonesia-lgbt-community-viewed-moral-threat.

Mohanty, Chandra Talpade, and Biddy Martin. 2003. "What's Home Got to Do with It?" In *Feminism without Borders: Decolonizing Theory, Practicing Solidarity*, edited by Chandra Talpade Mohanty, 85–105. Durham, NC: Duke University Press.

Moore, Henrietta L. 1994. *A Passion for Difference: Essays in Anthropology and Gender*. Bloomington: Indiana University Press.

Murray, Alison J. 1999. "Let Them Take Ecstasy: Class and Jakarta Lesbians." In *Female Desires: Same-Sex Relations and Transgender Practices across Cultures*, edited by Evelyn Blackwood and Saskia Wieringa, 139–56. New York: Columbia University Press.

Mustaghfiroh, Rahayu. 2014. "Constructing Sexuality in Panopticon *Pesantren*." In *Gender and Power in Indonesian Islam: Leaders, Feminists, Sufis, and Pesantren Selves*, edited by Bianca J. Smith and Mark Woodward, 175–86. London: Routledge.

Naafs, Suzanne. 2013. "Youth, Gender and the Workplace: Shifting Opportunities and Aspirations in an Indonesian Industrial Town." *Annals of the American Academy of Political and Social Science* 646 (1): 233–50.

Ngo, Jennifer. 2016. "Dr York Chow Bows Out as Hong Kong LGBT Community's Unlikeliest Champion." *South China Morning Post*, March 29. Accessed May 31, 2019. https://www.scmp.com/news/hong-kong/education-community/article/1931630/dr-york-chow-bows-out-hong-kong-lgbt-communitys.

Nikkei Asian Review. 2015. "Indonesians Splurge Wheb Monthly Income Passes $375." July 15. Accessed July 14, 2017. http://asia.nikkei.com/Business/Consumers/Indonesians-splurge-when-monthly-income-passes-375.

Nilan, Pam. 2008. "Youth Transitions to Urban, Middle-Class Marriage in Indonesia: Faith, Family and Finances." *Journal of Youth Studies* 11 (1): 65–82.

Nobles, Jenna, and Alison Buttenheim. 2008. "Marriage and Socioeconomic Change in Contemporary Indonesia." *Journal of Marriage and Family* 70 (4): 904–18.

Nurish, Amanah. 2010. "Women's Same-Sex Relations in Indonesian *Pesantren*." *Gender, Technology and Development* 14 (2): 267–77.

Nurmila, Nina. 2009. *Women, Islam and Everyday Life: Renegotiating Polygamy in Indonesia*. London: Routledge.

O'Connor, Paul. 2012. *Islam in Hong Kong: Muslims and Everyday Life in China's World City*. Hong Kong: Hong Kong University Press.

O'Connor, Paul. 2016. "Will You Eat Pork? Details of Domestic Workers on Public Display Raise Discrimination Concerns." *Hong Kong Free Press*, May 11. Accessed August 10, 2017. https://www.hongkongfp.com/2016/05/11/will-you-cook-pork-details-of-domestic-workers-on-public-display-raise-discrimination-concerns/.

Palmer, Wayne. 2010. "Costly Inducements." *Inside Indonesia*, April 24. Accessed September 29, 2018. http://www.insideindonesia.org/costly-inducements-2.

Parker, Lyn, and Pam Nilan. 2013. *Adolescents in Contemporary Indonesia*. New York: Routledge.

Parreñas, Rhacel Salazar. 2001. *Servants of Globalization: Women, Migration and Domestic Work*. Stanford, CA: Stanford University Press.

Pilkey, Brent, Rachael M. Scicluna, and Andrew Gorman-Murray. 2015. "Alternative Domesticities." *Home Cultures: The Journal of Architecture, Design and Domestic Space* 12 (2): 127–38.

Povinelli, Elizabeth A., and George Chauncey. 1999. "Thinking Sexuality Transnationally." *GLQ: A Journal of Lesbian and Gay Studies* 5 (4): 439–50.

Refworld. 2008. "Hong Kong: Situation and Treatment of Homosexuals; Availability of State Protection and Support Services (2005–May 2008)." Accessed May 31, 2019. https://www.refworld.org/docid/49b92b44c.html.

Rinaldo, Rachel. 2011. "Muslim Women, Moral Visions: Globalization and Gender Controversies in Indonesia." *Qualitative Sociology* 34: 539–60.

Robinson, Kathryn. 2000. "Gender, Islam, and Nationality: Indonesian Domestic Servants in the Middle East." In *Home and Hegemony: Domestic Service and Identity Politics in South and Southeast Asia*, edited by Kathleen M. Adams and Sara Dickey, 249–82. Ann Arbor: University of Michigan Press.

Robinson, Kathryn. 2009. *Gender, Islam and Democracy in Indonesia*. New York: Routledge.

Setyawati, Dinita. 2013. "Assets or Commodities? Comparing Regulations of Placement and Protection of Migrant Workers in Indonesia and the Philippines." *ASEAS-Austrian Journal of South-East Asian Studies* 6 (2): 264–80.

Shiraishi, Saya S. 1997. *Young Heroes: The Indonesian Family in Politics*. Ithaca, NY: Cornell Southeast Asia Program.

Silvey, Rachel. 2004. "Transnational Domestication: State Power and Indonesian Migrant Women in Saudi Arabia." *Political Geography* 23: 245–64.

Silvey, Rachel. 2006. "Consuming the Transnational Family: Indonesian Migrant Domestic Workers to Saudi Arabia." *Global Networks* 6 (1): 23–40.

Sim, Amy. 2009. *The Sexual Economy of Desire: Girlfriends, Boyfriends and Babies among Indonesian Women Migrants in Hong Kong*. Department of Sociology, University of Hong Kong. Accessed January 2, 2017. http://assets.publishing.service.gov.uk/media/57a08b7240f0b652dd000ca6/Sim_Sexual_Economy_of_Desire.pdf.

Sim, Amy. 2010. "Lesbianism among Indonesian Women Migrants in Hong Kong." In *As Normal As Possible: Negotiating Sexuality and Gender in Mainland China and Hong Kong*, edited by Yau Ching, 37–50. Hong Kong: Hong Kong University Press.

Sinnott, Megan. 2004. *Toms and Dees: Transgender Identity and Female Same-Sex Relationships in Thailand*. Honolulu: University of Hawai'i Press.

Situmorang, Augustina 2011. "Delayed Marriage among Lower Socio-economic Groups in an Indonesian Industrial City." In *Changing Marriage Patterns in Southeast Asia: Economic and Socio-cultural Dimensions*, edited by Gavin W. Jones, Terence H. Hull, and Maznah Mohamad, 83–98. London: Routledge.

Soewadi. 2012. "Lesbian dalam Pandangan Psikiatrik" [Lesbianism from a Psychiatric View]. *Tempo*, June 14. Accessed April 26, 2014. http://budisansblog.blogspot.com/2012/06/lesbian-dalam-pandangan-psikiatrik.html.

South China Morning Post. 2005. "Court Rules Age of Consent for Homosexuals Is Unconstitutional." August 24. Accessed June 1, 2019. https://www.scmp.com/print/article/513285/court-rules-age-consent-homosexuals-unconstitutional.

Straits Times. 2019a. "Meet Lini Zurlia, the Poster Girl for Protest Voting in Indonesia's Presidential Election." April 3. Accessed May 29, 2019. https://www.straitstimes.com/asia/se-asia/meet-lini-zurlia-the-poster-girl-for-protest-voting-in-indonesias-presidential-election.

Straits Times. 2019b. "Thousands Rally in Indonesia amid Controversial Criminal Code Changes." September 24. Accessed January 4, 2020. https://www.straitstimes.com/asia/se-asia/thousands-rally-in-indonesia-amid-controversial-criminal-code-changes.

Suen, Yiu-tung, Wai-ching Angela Wong, Amy Barrow, Miu-yin Wong, Wing-sze Winne Mak, Po-king Choi, Ching-man Lam, and Tak-fai Joseph Lau. 2016. *Study on Legislation against Discrimination on the Grounds of Sexual Orientation, Gender Identity and Intersex Status*. Hong Kong: Equal Opportunities Commission.

Time Out Hong Kong. 2012. "Girl-on-Girl Power." January 18–31. Accessed February 8, 2020. https://static1.squarespace.com/static/56a6ee9bd8af100c9a74d638/t/56c087e73c44d8d35d6a4431/1455458280496/96+LGBTI.pdf.

UNICEF. 2016. "State of The World's Children 2016 Country Statistical Information." Accessed April 28, 2017. https://data.unicef.org/resources/state-worlds-children-2016-statistical-tables/.

United Nations Committee on Economic, Social and Cultural Rights. 2001. *Consideration of Reports submitted by States Parties under Articles 16 and 17 of the Covenant, Concluding Observations of the Committee on Economic, Social and Cultural Rights: China: Hong Kong Special Administrative Region*. May 21. UN Doc E/C.12/1/Add.58.

United Nations Committee on Economic, Social and Cultural Rights. 2005. *Consideration of Reports submitted by States Parties under Articles 16 and 17 of the Covenant, Concluding Observations of the Committee on Economic, Social and Cultural Rights: People's Republic of China (including Hong Kong and Macao)*. May 13. UN Doc E/C.12/1/Add.107.

Valentine, Gill. 2007. "Theorizing and Researching Intersectionality: A Challenge for Feminist Geography." *Professional Geographer* 59 (1): 10–21.

Walton, Kate. 2013. "Caught between Two Happinesses." *Inside Indonesia*, August 30. Accessed June 29, 2018. http://www.insideindonesia.org/caught-between-two-happinesses?highlight=WyJsZXNiaWFuIiwiJ2xlc2JpYW4nLiIsIidsZXNiaWFuJyIsIidsZXNiaWFuJywiXQ%3D%3D.

Warouw, Nicolaas. 2008. "Industrial Workers in Transition: Women's Experiences of Factory Work in Tangerang." In *Women and Work in Indonesia*, edited by Michele Ford and Lyn Parker, 104–19. London: Routledge.

Wee, Vivienne, and Amy Sim. 2005. "Hong Kong as a Destination for Migrant Domestic Workers." In *Asian Women as Transnational Domestic Workers*, edited by Shirlena Huang, Brenda S. A. Yeoh, and Noor Abdul Rahman, 175–209. Singapore: Marshall Cavendish.

Weiss, Margot. 2016. "Always After: Desiring Queerness, Desiring Anthropology." *Cultural Anthropology* 31 (4): 627–38.

Wekker, Gloria. 2006. *The Politics of Passion: Women's Sexual Culture in the Afro-Surinamese Diaspora*. New York: Columbia University Press.

Wieringa, Saskia E. 2007. "'If There Is No Feeling . . .': The Dilemma between Silence and Coming Out in a Working-Class Butch/Femme Community in Jakarta." In *Love and Globalization: Transformations of Intimacy in the Contemporary World*, edited by Mark B. Padilla, Jennifer S. Hirsch, Miguel Munoz-Laboy, Robert E. Sember and Richard G. Parker, 70–90. Nashville, TN: Vanderbilt University Press.

Wieringa, Saskia E. 2012. "Passionate Aesthetics and Symbolic Subversion: Heteronormativity in India and Indonesia." *Asian Studies Review* 36 (4): 515–30. https://doi.org/10.1080/10357823.2012.739997.

Wieringa, Saskia E. 2015. "Gender Harmony and the Happy Family: Islam, Gender and Sexuality in Post-Reformasi Indonesia." *South East Asia Research* 23 (1): 27–44.

Wieringa, Saskia E. 2017. "Indonesian University Prohibits LGBT Students to Register." *Amsterdam Research Centre for Gender and Sexuality* (blog). May 14. Accessed May 14, 2017. http://arcgs.uva.nl/content/blog/researchers-blog/wieringa.html?origin=suTDpgBbQbOQZdoPdn3Rug?.

Wieringa, Saskia, Abha Bhaiya, and Nursyahbani Katjasungkana. 2015. *Heteronormativity, Passionate Aesthetics and Symbolic Subversion in Asia*. Brighton: Susses Academic Press

WKNews. 2015. "「我們是同志，我們很好」外傭舉辦首屆同志遊行" ["We are queer, we are fabulous," migrant workers held their first Pride March]. Novermber 11. Accessed June 5, 2017. http://wknews.org/node/928.

Wong, Angela W. C. 2013. "The Politics of Sexual Morality and Evangelical Activism in Hong Kong." *Inter-Asia Cultural Studies* 14 (3): 340–60.

Yeoh, Brenda S. A., and Shirlena Huang. 1998. "Negotiating Public Space: Strategies and Styles of Migrant Female Domestic Workers in Singapore." *Urban Studies* 35 (3): 583–602.

Yeoh, Brenda S. A., and Shirlena Huang . 2010. "Transnational Domestic Workers and the Negotiation of Mobility and Work Practices in Singapore's Home-Spaces." *Mobilities* 5 (2): 219–36.

Index

agency 3, 17, 86
Ardhanary Institute 26
Asian Migrants Coordinating Body 32
Association for the Advancement of Feminism 32

bisexuality 4
Blackwood, Evelyn 6, 10, 15, 25, 50, 69, 104
Boellstorff, Tom 5, 10, 27–28, 43
Bourdieu, Pierre 54
brokers 21
Butler, Judith 75

cewek, defined 13, 42
cities, imagining of 108–10
citizenship 7, 27, 43
class: 5–6, 109; lower-class 94, 116; middle-class 84; treatment 97, 99
coming out 2, 10, 36, 53
Constable, Nicole 3, 8–9, 20–21, 23–25, 29, 34, 38, 40, 63, 78, 84
cuma di sini (only here) 82–83

dance groups 13, 38–42; competition 43–44, 46
divorce 17, 24, 107, 113
doa (short prayer) 85
dog, taking care of 81
Dunia Kita 32, 35

Espín, Oliva 7–8

family: causes of working abroad 56–58, 61; facilitating labor migration 21; family honor 7, 83; family-ism (kekeluargaan) 47; girlfriends' children 112–14; marriage pressure 115–17; materialistic satisfaction 22; moving away 108; relationship with husband and children 107; relationship with parents 105–6; unmarried daughters' status 22; transnational family 1
fashion show 42–46, 86
femininity: at employer's home 93; in a relationship 69–70; gender shifting 75
feminization of labor migration 1, 19–20, 121–22, 124
field methods 12–14; ethics 16; researcher's sexuality 13–16
Filguys Association 31, 36
Filipino Lesbian Organization 31
Foucault, Michel 51–53

Gabriela 32
gay liberation model 1, 10, 111
gender: gender ambiguity 94–96; gender binary 42–46; gender discourses 21–25; gender identity outweigh sexual identity 7; gender perspective 2; gender shifting 74–76; when praying 85–86

Hari Raya Idul Fitri 67, 86
heteronormativity: defined 6; home 104; labor migration policies 5; subversion of 5, 103, 114; surveillance 8, 10

Index

home: imaginings of 9–11, 108–10; Indonesian discourse 21–22; power dynamics 102; queer home 53; remaking the space of home 111–14
homonormativity 5
Hong Kong employers 8, 34–36; abuse 23; at employer's home 8, 92–94; discriminated by 32, 95; gendered expectations 96; sexual threat 34, 93–94; types of household 72
Hong Kong government 29
Hong Kong laws: employment ordinance 89; immigration ordinance 102
Hong Kong Pride Parade 29, 32

Indonesian government: anti-LGBT 26–28; foreign remittance 19; reconciling Islamic expectations with overseas work 79–80
Indonesian laws: marriage law 107; placement and protection for Indonesian overseas workers 21, 80; pornography law 27
Institut Pelangi Perempuan 26
intersectionality 6–8, 78
Islam: conflicts with overseas work 80–83; Islamic conservatism 19, 27–28; Islamic law 8–9, 27; men's Islamic clothing 33, 88; new interpretation 86–88; religious subjectivity 9; shelters 89–91; unclean 83–84; women's Islamic clothing 8, 33, 85, 90

Jilbab: defined 8; in rural areas 59, 84; middle-class young women 84; not allowed by employer 9

kin world: dance groups 47; intelligibility 75–76; kin labor 48–50
Kowloon Park 39
Kwai Chung Plaza 45

labor issues 49, 89
Left 21 32
lesbian: avoiding the word 112; communities in Indonesia 104; lesbian friend in Indonesia 106; media report 33–35; migrants 7–8, 10, 31–32; researcher 13; sexual disorder 25; sinful 33, 82

LGBT movements: anti-LGBT 27–28, 30, 33; Hong Kong 29; Indonesia 26; judicial reviews 30; migrant domestic workers 31–32; public attitudes toward homosexuality 30
Lindquist, Johan 2, 21, 23, 51

Manalansan, Martin 2, 5, 7, 10, 103, 109
marriage: bogus marriage 66; extramarital affairs 3, 24, 88, 107; family expectation 10, 118–19; fiancé in Indonesia 17, 74; ideal path 117; relationship with husband 107; rite of passage 115; sexual reputation 23; strategy of resistance 117–19
men: Hong Kong men 39, 66; Indonesian men 39, 60–63; South Asian men 39, 63
men's underwear 95–96
migrant activism 40, 46
migrant community: site of resistance 38; Sunday activities 38–40; membership-based groups 41
Migrants Pride March 32
Moore, Henrietta 54
motherhood 21; in dance group 50; parenting a girlfriend's children 113–14; relationship with children 107

nakal (naughty) 82–83, 90

pesantren (Islamic boarding schools) 51
pork 8–9, 78–81, 87
pregnancy 3, 33, 51, 65
prestasi (achievement) 43
prison studies 51

queer: subject position 4–6; possibilities of queerness 5, 124; queer studies 9, 123
queer migration 2, 3, 7, 109

Ramadan 86
recruitment agencies 21, 49, 80

salat 84–85, 87–89
same-sex relationships 2, 10, 11; desiring a same-sex relationship 67–69; justifying same-sex relationships 82–84; pampering 69, 74; projecting a stuffed animal as their child 73–74; visibility of same-sex relationship 38, 42; wedding 35, 73
Sector 15 of Koalisi Perempuan Indonesia 26
sex between two women 57, 74
sexual fluidity 4
sexual orientation 4, 36
Sim, Amy 3, 21, 35, 51
single mothers 24–25
structural inequality 7
Swara Srikandi 26

Taiwan: 3, 23, 29, 65
tomboi: at employer's home 93; fashion show 42–47, 86; in a relationship 55–59, 69–74; in Padang 6; meanings of 8, 50–53

training centers 20, 50–51, 55–59, 61, 80–81
transnational feminism 3
transnational sexuality 123

unmarried women: ambivalent future 117–19; overseas employment 24; wanting to get married 115–16
urbanization 104

Victoria Park 14, 39–40, 47, 85, 93

Waria, defined 75
widow 17
Wieringa, Saskia 5–6, 10, 25, 27–28, 104, 111–12

www.ingramcontent.com/pod-product-compliance
Ingram Content Group UK Ltd.
Pitfield, Milton Keynes, MK11 3LW, UK
UKHW021831210426
5322IPUK00004B/139